MANAGING VOLUNTEERS EFFECTIVELY

Managing Volunteers Effectively

Phil McSweeney
Don Alexander

Published by
Arena
Ashgate Publishing Limited
Gower House
Croft Road
Aldershot
Hants GU11 3HR
England

Ashgate Publishing Company
Old Post Road
Brookfield
Vermont 05036
USA

British Library Cataloguing in Publication Data

McSweeney, Phil
  Managing volunteers effectively
  1. Volunteers 2. Voluntarism – Management
  3. Voluntarism – Personnel management
  I. Title   II. Alexander, Don
  361.3´7´0683

Library of Congress Catalog Card Number: 96–84014

  ISBN 1 85742 293 7 (paperback)
  ISBN 1 85742 294 5 (hardback)

Typeset in Palatino by Raven Typesetters Ltd, Chester.
Printed and bound in Great Britain by Hartnolls Ltd, Bodmin.

Contents

About the authors

Phil McSweeney has worked in the National Health Service for much of his working life and, with all the reorganisations it has undergone, he knows a little about change! He has been a nurse, a clinical manager, a teacher and researcher, and in senior management. He currently works as a Performance and Strategy Manager for a health authority and is involved in commissioning high quality cost-effective services from statutory service providers and from not-for-profit and voluntary agencies. More recently he has provided training and consultancy to these. His various working roles have given him a great deal of experience with people, and he finds that his past work as a teacher enables him to communicate ideas easily to people. He holds an MA in Sociological Research in Health Care at the University of Warwick and completed an MBA at the University of Essex in 1992. Phil has particularly firm views about the importance of delivering quality services and has included many modern management ideas in this book.

Don Alexander has many years' personal experience as a volunteer and as a teacher and researcher of voluntary sector policy and practice. He is a qualified and experienced teacher, counsellor and nurse, having worked for several years as a service manager within the NHS prior to moving into education. He has taught community and voluntary sector courses within a range of higher education establishments and has worked as an education manager. His first degree is in Social Science in which he majored in social policy and the management of welfare. In 1992 he gained his Master's degree in Sociology and Social Policy, researching the volunteer's role in implementing care in the community and the implicit management changes required. Following this he has worked for two national voluntary organisations managing and developing care in the community.

The authors have previously worked together on course development and delivery in higher education. Their collaboration has ranged across vocational, developmental and policy appreciation courses of various lengths, both for volunteers and managers. In the last three years the authors have worked together utilising their complementary skills to deliver contemporary management training, consultancy, facilitation and development to volunteers and managers in-house.

Introduction

This book is probably for you. How do we know this? Well, first, we've written it because we're convinced the time is right. The pace of change in society continues to accelerate more rapidly and there is no doubt that every voluntary organisation is feeling the pace of change in its own way. A growing array of social, technological, environmental and political factors are making increasing demands on voluntary organisations and at the same time threatening to outstrip their ability to respond.

These change factors are felt in many ways. In the UK people of all ages are increasingly in need of information, counsel, practical help or financial advice to cope with the growing complexity of contemporary life. Overseas, the demands are greater and even more basic. Much of this demand will impact on charities and voluntary organisations. If you are a volunteer or a manager in a voluntary organisation you will already have some idea of where your particular pressures are coming from. We believe that you, and people like you, could use some extra help – a resourceful book such as this to help you manage through those changes.

However, not just any management book will do. Our experience tells us that there are a great deal of special factors to take into account in trying to manage in the voluntary sector, some of which are poorly recognised. How can you get the best out of volunteers, whether they are phone-manning or fundraising? How can you develop strategies and work collaboratively with other agencies using volunteers? How can you sift through all the wider commercial management ideas to see if any apply in your sector? How can you lead your largely voluntary team through some of your proliferating agenda items? How will you deliver against a contract with such a team? Where will you find the time to invest in making yourself more effective at these activities?

Consider the pressing example of the increased expectations placed upon many voluntary organisations by the implementation of the Community Care Act in 1993. Our society is changing both in structure and in attitude – an obvious example being the growing number of elderly people who will need some support to stay in their own homes. The Act moves local authorities away from direct welfare provision to being an 'enabler and purchaser' of services. It requires local authorities to develop a mixed economy for the provision of community care. There is an explicit expectation that voluntary organisations will participate in making care in the community work effectively. Community care will be given in an increasing variety of ways, many of which will be pioneered by the voluntary services. It is implicit in the contract culture that it will not suffice for voluntary organisations to raise funds for community care – they are expected to actively participate.

There are many other examples of how changes in society are impacting on charities' workload. National charities such as Help the Aged, Shelter, Relate, Save the Children, the NSPCC and the Samaritans are experiencing increased demand. Overseas, war, poverty and hunger are currently placing massive demands upon Oxfam, the Red Cross, VSO and the like in Eastern Europe and parts of Africa. Closer to home pressures are growing on local charitable and voluntary organisations whether in youth work, childcare, drug abuse, animal welfare, housing, advocacy or environmental issues. The specific roles of volunteers may differ in these different organisations but the challenges for management remain broadly constant. One of the most important has to be how to manage volunteers effectively. Many voluntary organisations now readily accept that, to thrive, they have to invest in such skills as the finer arts of marketing and fundraising. We believe voluntary organisations will increasingly come to realise that they will have to pay more attention to managing volunteers.

We are painting a picture in which many voluntary organisations find that, with the increasing pressures and demands made on them, they do not have the resources to keep pace neither with the needs they identify nor their aspirations. As a manager you may be faced with the challenge of an increasingly difficult task – that of getting the best out of a special group of people, volunteers, who themselves are a limited resource. If this picture looks familiar, this book is for you!

We had two reasons for writing this book. The first has been concerned with helping managers in voluntary organisations to respond to the great changes ahead and the need to equip them with skills to deliver their objectives through better management of volunteers. The second reason is not dissimilar but is more internally focused on the competence of management itself. There have been public cases which have questioned this, the most famous recently being the insolvency of War on Want in 1990. The Charity Commission Inquiry which followed exposed many grave deficiencies in the administration of the charity, as well as financial irregularities and unresolved internal disputes. Management in the voluntary sector is becoming an increasingly pressured activity. The new Charities Act, funding applications, VAT, employment legislation, auditing requirements, equal opportunities, negotiating new contracts, cuts in traditional sources of money ... all are taking their toll on managers' time and skills.

Management in charities and voluntary organisations is undergoing a great transition. In 1977 the National Council for Voluntary Organisations (NCVO) asked management guru, Charles Handy, to lead a working party to look at voluntary sector management. This led to a Working Party Report and the establishment of the NCVO Management Development Unit. Handy has since published his *Understanding Voluntary Organisations* (1988), and the NCVO has continued to be active in advancing good management and providing training for trustees.

Handy's work opened up the culture clash between the management 'old guard' and the new professionals. Handy made two allegations of management in the voluntary sector – 'strategic delinquency' or putting ethos before strategy, and the 'servant syndrome', making virtues of shabbiness and parsimony. The new professionals view the 'old guard' stereotypically as well intentioned relics of an amateur past, who frustrate progress, often because of their trustee status. On the other hand the conservative elders tend to view the 'flashy' methods of the new professionals – direct mailshots, colour brochures, media and corporate entertainment – with disdain, if not as sacrilege. As a manager of volunteers you are likely to find yourself in the midst of this tension between the progressive and sometimes brash push and the need to preserve a traditional and compassionate image. Making sense of this for yourself, and more importantly for volunteers, will be a challenge as will the need to temper and negotiate with one or other of these influences.

So we've written this book as a resource. We have aimed it at people in management positions anywhere in the voluntary sector, for those who'd like to move into a more managerial role or even for those who feel they could help their managers manage a little better! Doing something worthwhile in voluntary work is a fine goal in itself. Being committed to your organisation's principles is fine too. But if you feel you'd like to achieve a little more at work through better management, to get a little more out of your team through better teamwork, then this book will help you do that. Sometimes it may just help you get through the day!

You might be in a paid position in a voluntary organisation or a volunteer yourself. You might be thinking about a career move into a voluntary organisation or might have taken early retirement. You might be working with a statutory organisation, such as social services, that wants to discover ways of working more closely with the voluntary sector. You may have had some management or supervisory experience in a previous organisation –

possibly even some management training – or, alternatively you may be entirely new to management. Whatever your experience we aim to put across to you some straightforward management principles in such a way that you will be able to put them to immediate use. We will help you to apply them particularly in the volunteer context. You might consider that volunteers who give their time freely and for the reward of the work itself may be deserving of good management. Can you make it any better?

There is no doubt that the UK charities sector is healthy in terms of growth. It has a turnover of around £17 billion from donations, endowments, grants and interest earnings, and employs some 4 per cent of the nation's workforce. The annual income of the top four charities exceeds £50 million each: the National Trust at £78 million, Oxfam at £59 million, the RNLI at £56 million and the Save the Children Fund at £53 million. There are over 170 000 registered charities and a new one is registered every hour of the working day. Over 12 500 were registered in 1994 alone.

There is no doubt that there has been an explosion in management thinking in the last decade too. But, somehow, these two growth paths haven't always crossed. Have you experienced the constantly recurring agenda item, the 'pass the parcel' decision that is never made, or paralysis by analysis? Have you discovered the job that you thought was finished but everybody thought someone else was doing? We've found that even quite experienced managers in other settings often need help to tune their management skills to this area of work. We've tried to address some of the gaps you may have in managing in this sector and to make this book a really valuable handbook for tackling some everyday management problems. We think you'll find much here to improve your effectiveness.

From the contents page you'll see this book follows an easy and logical structure. It begins with a few reminders of common management themes and emphasises the skills all managers need to be more effective and efficient. Chapter 2, as you might expect, then explores the theme of change in our society, mainly from the perspective of the effects of social and political changes where the changes for the voluntary sector are most significant. The contract culture – the new way of doing business between the voluntary and statutory sectors – is one example. We take the view that good managers achieve change by managing it proactively rather than being overwhelmed by it.

Chapter 3 helps you to understand what your organisation is trying to achieve – its purpose, mission, vision and values. How often do you find yourself asking such questions as: 'What's the point of all this?', 'What are we trying to achieve here?' or 'Are we all going in the same direction, at the same time?' Are you clear about your role in that task and that direction? Would it be of benefit if you could help volunteers to see your organisation's mission more clearly? Being clear about purpose is crucial to planning and fundraising activities, both of which are discussed in the book.

Chapters 4 to 6 focus on skills in managing yourself and managing volunteers both as individuals and in teams. We help you analyse your own strengths and weaknesses, to recognise and manage stress more effectively and to improve your use of that very limited resource – time itself. We explore the particular needs of volunteers and ways of providing them with support and motivation. Getting the best out of volunteers by a better understanding of what to look for in effective groups and how to address teamwork problems are the final themes in these three chapters.

Some particular 'recruit and retain' issues are dealt with in Chapter 7. Staff selection and retention is becoming a more pressing issue. While everyone has views on what makes volunteers special, they could also benefit from advice on selecting, keeping and developing them. Moreover, when working with the public, it will become increasingly important to be able to demonstrate the safest selection processes.

Increasingly, many successful organisations are attributing their success to attending to quality, which in turn means meeting the needs of customers. Historically the voluntary sector can pride itself in being very responsive to the needs of its 'customers', but consumerism is growing and people are becoming more vocal about what they want. The Citizen's Charter is having an effect here, and statutory organisations may also be beginning to be better at listening. For consumers, the ability to deliver will increasingly become the yardstick by which all organisations are measured. Chapter 8 therefore looks at ways of pleasing the customer.

Finally the book ends with a review of some of the key themes presented and some good ideas in taking them forward in everyday practice. You will find some useful items in the Appendices such as how to write a short report, construct your CV or give a short presentation.

We've taken the view that, first, you'll get most out of the book by buying it! This is not intended to sound facetious. We sincerely hope you will treat it as an investment in yourself and your work. Next, and once you own it, don't be afraid to interact with it. To illustrate many of the key ideas we offer a range of case studies, exercises and activities which we're sure you'll enjoy. From the range of material here and the approach we've taken in introducing it, we're sure you'll find this book invaluable. Don't feel that you need to read it from start to finish; dip into those chapters where you feel a need. Finally, try to put some of it into practice. Don't be afraid to try out some of the ideas you like. You'll find that you can enjoy becoming a better manager!

Good luck and enjoy the journey.

Phil McSweeney
Don Alexander

1 Me: the manager

Yes, you! You're a manager and there's no going back! Whether you're new to the position or have years of experience you'll have some ideas about management. We hope we can share some ideas about management with you which may challenge yours and make you think, particularly in the area of working with volunteers.

We also believe that there is no better time than the present. Management is not getting any easier, and the world is not slowing down. Special skills are going to be needed in the voluntary sector if it is to continue to achieve its wide range of purposes with any continuing degree of success. If you are new there is plenty to see and learn about. If you are not so new then it might be a good time to take an objective look at what you've been doing all these years! We'll start by revisiting some first principles.

First principles

Myths about management

Some people say managers are born not made, and therefore it's no use trying to learn to be a better one. As teachers by background we believe that everyone has unfulfilled potential. We believe that, given the right support, people can develop skills in almost any endeavour. What may be more true is that some people have learnt how to learn from their own experience better than others. We learn whether we are getting better at something by being better attuned to the feedback we receive and by being more reflective about what happened when we did something. For that reason we have adopted a style of asking you questions – to promote your reflection on what you've learnt.

Another common myth about management is that all management is

1

common sense. If it is, there are a great many people making a living out of telling us what we probably already know. Moreover, one person's common sense is not the same as another's. People might hold some beliefs or views in common with most of their fellow staff, but having similar views will not guarantee that people will act in the same way. If you asked a group of ten people to meet at a venue at 6p.m., there would be some who would be early, some who would be late, one would probably get lost, they'd all go by different routes, park in different places, some would bring a pen and some not, and so on. If you asked them why they did what they did they'd probably say it was common sense!

Common sense is that property you expect people to have, which makes them behave the same as you would in any given situation. Clearly they don't, because everyone has their own individual perspectives about the best way to do something. It would be more true to say that giving people management training might improve their 'common' sense by equipping them with more analytical ways of looking at problems and leading them to better solutions.

The next great myth is that if management isn't all common sense then it's just about implementing a few more or less constant rules of thumb that will stand you in good stead through thick and thin. Theories about management as a comprehensive art or science have been around for about a hundred years. During that time there have been some fairly enduring principles about management, but there has also been an ebb and flow of fashionable ideas. We have moved from the rational, scientific 'one best way' approaches to the contingent 'it all depends on the circumstances' or 'best fit' approaches. We have swung back and forth from systems views of management to human resources views. Views *do* change over time and we have to be willing to test new ideas. You will, however, find that large parts of management theory are relatively easy to follow and are often within your experience after all. It's not all the equivalent of rocket science!

There is something comforting about rocket science though. It is less open to question. For such phenomena as 'flight' or 'internal combustion' or 'lack of oxygen' one theory usually suffices for years. These theories have a concreteness about them; they either work or they do not. Unfortunately management theory, being a 'soft' science, is not so easy to pin down. The relative dearth of formal management education usually means that most of our theories are 'homespun' or developed from our own experience. Most managers have learnt to manage by the 'seat of their pants', which further tends to undermine the fact that there is anything of substance to learn.

Good communication

Some people have the same views about management as they do about communication – that you're either good at it or not or, again, it's all common sense. But imagine what it would be like working in the 'all communication is common sense' organisation. One plus factor would be that there would be very few arguments. We could all get on quietly with our jobs, mostly without telling anybody else what we were doing and why – because it would be common sense to us all. Yet, if anything, common sense might tell us we should improve our communications. The following short exercise might illustrate this point.

Exercise 1.1   Good and poor managers

Think about a 'good' manager you have known and also a 'poor' manager.
List the things the 'good' manager did well that made you believe he or she was a good manager.

Now list the things the 'poor' manager did poorly that made you believe he or she was a poor manager.

In your list we would predict that you'll have mentioned something to do with communication or information. Check these against the items in the list below.

Good manager	*Poor manager*
Easy to talk to	Difficult to talk to
Good listener	Didn't listen to me
Gave me clear direction about what to do	Gave me little direction about what to do
Shared information with me	Didn't share information with me
Usually available for advice	Couldn't find them sometimes
Shared their goals with me	Didn't tell me their goals
Replied promptly to my memos/messages	Always chasing them for answers

Can you rate the way you communicate as consistently good or do you tend towards some of the poor qualities listed?

In addition to these general communication skills you need to consider the special requirements for communicating with volunteers. Because you see them much less frequently the methods you use to communicate with them will be different to those you use with your day-to-day colleagues. Your communication will need more planning and forethought.

Exercise 1.2   Effective communication methods?

List your most usual methods for communicating with volunteers. How effective do you think these are?

How do you know how effective they are? Have you asked any of the volunteers? How about asking one or two?

A recent Industrial Society survey of 1000 organisations found the two most effective methods of communication with employees to be *team briefings* and *walking the job* (Carrington, 1994).

Team briefings involve getting your team together to give them detailed directions about what is happening or what needs doing, encouraging questions and checking their understanding. Because the meetings should be interactive some organisations now call them *team talks*.

Walking the job literally means leaving your desk to go and talk with those doing the 'nuts and bolts' work, finding out how they are coping and what problems they've got. It implies being seen to be interested in volunteers.

Team briefings and walking the job are both good examples of ways you can improve communication with volunteers. But by communication we don't just mean telling volunteers what *you* want. We mean a proper two-way communication of each other's positions on matters of concern, demonstrating that you are listening. Good communication is a sharing of meaning between each party – a process of reaching a clear understanding between you. Obviously you need to hold team briefings at a time and place convenient to most volunteers. If they miss them, how do they find out what was discussed – second-hand or by Chinese whispers? It is helpful to write down some briefing notes, making sure that these are clear and unambiguous. Do you also go and see volunteers while they are working? It is another opportunity for both them and you to achieve a better understanding of each other's situation. We will return again and again in this book to the vital and all-pervasive theme of good communication as a prerequisite for successful management.

Efficiency and effectiveness

Those items you listed in Exercises 1.1 and 1.2 represent some of your views or theories about what makes a manager effective or not. Two very important qualities are frequently mentioned together in management theory: the two 'E's – effectiveness and efficiency. Effectiveness is best understood as doing the right things, whereas efficiency is making the most economical use of resources. Effectiveness is more important than efficiency because first of all one must be doing the right kind of work. Only then does it matter whether the work is done efficiently (after Stewart, 1985).

We could use Stewart's view to attempt to define management in simple terms: *good managers get the right job done well*. In a people-intensive arena, such as the voluntary sector, we might usefully add to this definition: *good management is getting people to do the right job well or properly*. Effectiveness and efficiency – are you doing the right job and are you doing it right? Are there different ways to be effective and efficient? Or is it all common sense? Perhaps that's the value of developing management skills.

The wood and the trees

You will certainly not be alone in the realisation that what you are actually doing and what you should be doing have become a little detached from each other. One aspect of being effective is being able to cope with the present and simultaneously plan for the future. This has been described variously as 'seeing the wood from the trees', managing both for maintenance and development or having 'helicopter vision'. The next exercise takes you on an imaginary journey to help you attain a clearer view of your job.

Exercise 1.3   The helicopter ride

Tomorrow morning instead of going to work you will be picked up by our helicopter. We shall spend the day hovering over where you usually work, where your team works, where your boss works, your head office, your whole organisation. We shall watch your department and every other department going about its daily business, seeing how they all interlink and communicate with each other. We shall watch how effective you and all the others are, whether you are doing the right thing, whether you all seem to have purpose in what you are doing, whether all your customers are getting what they expect and what you have promised.

We're sure we could look at many interesting things from up there, and you could possibly suggest a few too. Take your time to think about those we've listed below.

Who are the good managers? What are they doing that marks them out from the others? Who needs help?

We could look at who is making the most effective and efficient use of their volunteers. What are they doing differently to you or the others? Are their volunteers different in any way?

We could form a view about whether the whole organisation is ticking over nicely (or not) and what needs to change. What would be the first thing you would improve?

More challengingly we could fly higher and take a look at the horizon. What is coming your way? How soon? Do you see these as opportunities or threats? How well prepared are you and your team for these changes?

Now back to solid ground! This exercise is called a 'visioning' exercise which you can do as often as you like to help you see the whole wood – not always easy when you spend a lot of time deep in the undergrowth! However, merely glimpsing the whole picture may only give temporary relief or frustrate you further. To manage better you need to maintain a clear view of the future. Some would say that management is all about future planning. You can't change the past and you can't change much that is going on in the present, but if you have a clear view of your destination you can steer towards it.

Whilst you might agree with having this outlook you might also find it very difficult to see beyond the day-to-day bombardment of issues thrown at you. We sometimes refer to this as the 'difficult to find your way out of the swamp when you are up to your armpits in alligators' perspective. This book will equip you with skills to improve your 'helicopter vision'.

What managers do

Many theorists could help us here, but we will call on Mintzberg. Using observational techniques Mintzberg and others have studied what managers actually do as opposed to what the theories say they should do. Several would agree with his findings that manager's jobs are characterised by pace, interruptions, brevity, variety and fragmentation of activities, and a preference for verbal contacts (Pugh and Hickson, 1989:32). He found among managers what he called the 'ten minute itch'. Almost everything they do, apart from meetings, seems to fit into approximate ten-minute bursts of time – scan a report or two, dash off a couple of letters, keep an appointment, make a few brief calls, take a quick walk round the patch and so on. You might recognise yourself here, but remember, pace and variety alone don't assure good management, only that you haven't time to get bored! All that fragmented activity is supposed to add up to something deliberate and purposeful.

Mintzberg theorises that there are ten key roles to management. He groups these into three areas:

- **Interpersonal:** the relationships that you have to have with others.
- **Informational:** how you use information to manage.

● **Decisional:** the different roles in which you make decisions.

The ten roles outlined within each of these areas are as follows:

● **Interpersonal:**

- figurehead: how you use your position to represent your organisation
- leader: how you take people along with you
- liaison: the networks you establish internally and externally.

● **Informational:**

- monitor: keeping in touch with what goes on both within and outside the organisation
- disseminator: passing information on
- spokesperson: giving information to people outside the organisation.

● **Decisional:**

- entrepreneur: the good ideas you have about change and what you do with them
- disturbance-handler: how you deal with the unpredicted
- resource-allocator: how you share out equipment, money, staff, time and so on
- negotiator: how you try to get what you want or need.

The mix and balance of these roles vary from job to job and may need to change as your organisation changes. Are there any that you think are most critical to managing volunteers effectively? We have already highlighted communication in all its forms as a key activity, and that is well represented in Mintzberg's analysis.

The exercise below gives you a more structured way of thinking about Mintzberg's roles.

Exercise 1.4   Mintzberg roles and your job

Try to identify at least one of the usual activities in your job that matches each of Mintzberg's roles below. Make a note of it and identify, where possible, those which relate directly to managing volunteers.

1   **Informational**

● monitor

- disseminator
- spokesperson.

2   **Interpersonal**

- figurehead
- leader
- liaiser.

3   **Decisional**

- entrepreneur
- disturbance-handler
- resource-allocator
- negotiator.

Most managers should be able to identify some of their activities against most of the roles Mintzberg gives. You may find many more in some roles than others but this may be because your job is 'shaped' like that. But this exercise should help you to assess whether you've got the balance right, or whether there is a role in which you are not performing well and on which you need to improve. This sometimes occurs immediately after a job change. You need to deliberately think through how you should change the balance of these roles to do your new job effectively.

Example: Don's changed role

When Don moved from being a senior lecturer in a college to a manager in a voluntary organisation he had to stop himself from thinking about how to generate income from developing and marketing courses. He also had to think about how he would motivate volunteers in a particular project. He therefore had to perform his entrepreneurial role differently and develop his leadership, figurehead and disturbance-handler roles.

New to management?

What if you've just been promoted or are new to management? Have you made the adjustments not only to your new role but also to your new status? Most of your previous experience of your new role will be from the perspective of the 'managed' rather than of the manager. You may also have difficulties in letting go of the responsibilities of your previous job. You may feel drawn to the safety of continuing to try to do parts of it or keeping very involved with it. Beware of falling into the 'player–manager syndrome'.

The player–manager

The following case study explains this syndrome. It describes how Don Alexander (a fictitious character) became involved in his new job as Branch Manager at the Recycled Rubbish charity. After you have read through it, identify ways in which Don has failed to recognise the demands of his new job as compared with his previous one.

Case study: Oh, no! It's Don Alexander, the player–manager!

Don Alexander is a Branch Manager for Recycled Rubbish in Rutland. Each county has a branch with a network of volunteers. They collect rubbish, sort it in various categories, sell it to various dealers with whom they have established contracts and distribute the returns to the top three charities voted for by the volunteer members. Distribution and voting takes place each year. A new set of three charities is selected every year as well.

Recycled Rubbish has been established for ten years. It appeals to volunteers who want to give tangible help as a large donation to charities they select, and assists conservation by recycling waste.

Each branch of the charity usually has five teams – Paper and Board, Glass, Tin Cans, Valuables and Miscellaneous. Each team sets its own strategy with guidelines from the Branch Manager. Usually this means that the first three – Paper, Glass and Tins – establish regular collection points, and Valuables asks for donations or offers free house clearance. Good Miscellaneous teams set up the most diverse and imaginative activities, from organised 'bin dives' and visiting rubbish tips to metal detector outings. A 'bin dive' involves finding out when someone has a good skip full of rubbish outside their house and asking whether a Recycling 'snatch squad' can come and pick through it.

Six months ago Don – previously Tin Can team leader – had successfully applied for the Branch Manager's job. The previous Branch Manager had retired unexpectedly after a metal detector outing where he claimed to have found one George III gold coin that he handed to the Valuables team leader. This had since been auctioned for £3000. Three months later the Branch Manager had declared he was moving to his villa in Tuscany, which nobody knew about, and he was gone.

Don was pleased to get the job with a small salary as he had been nudged into early retirement in his previous job as a milk roundsman. As Tin Can team leader he had been an excellent resource, finding out from the milk round who had had a skip delivered, who was moving house, who had recently died and so on and feeding all that 'intelligence' into his branch. He used to keep a large box in the cab of his float which, with vigilance, he could usually fill with tins and bottles twice a week from his round. In the six years since he'd been team leader of the Tin Can team they'd exceeded their collection total every year and were well up in the counties league, despite Rutland's small size. He was valued by the previous Branch Manager for his enthusiasm, and he had felt that he could enthuse the whole branch with his ideas and methods.

It was difficult taking over with no handover period. He tried hard to continue gathering 'information' by noticing things when he was driving around. He tried to fill the box he kept in his car by calling at some of his usual sources regularly. He arranged to go out with the other teams to see what they were doing and inject some more enthusiasm into them. He ended up having an argument with the Valuables team leader who felt his ideas were not appropriate.

His enthusiasm to keep the teams on the job seemed to become a bit wearing. Team leaders and volunteers didn't turn up at the new meetings he arranged with them. One or two of the house owners who had collection points started to phone up to say that paper or bottles were stacking up and they were no longer routinely picked up. He resolved this by doing most of these pick-ups on his way home.

Don's work office had started to pile up, and one or two letters had gone astray. Last week he had lost the date of a country fair with which the Recyclers had a standing arrangement to clear up afterwards. Today, he feels under a great deal of pressure. He has just had a letter from the Regional Manager saying she would like to come over in two days' time to see how he was settling in. 'By the way' the letter continued, 'could I also point out that I have not received your county ballot papers for next year's charity choices. I would like to pick them up on my visit as the deadline is the following day.' Don flew into a panic! Two hundred and thirty ballot papers to collect from all volunteers and officers within two days and his part-time secretary tells him he hasn't yet asked her to send them out!

Taking on this management job isn't turning out quite as he thought it would. Being a team leader had been easy and fun. This is just one big headache!

Can you see where Don is having problems? What should he stop doing and what should he do more of? He must think through his new role and define his new objectives. He should try to give others some of the roles he used to take on himself.

Perhaps you know a manager who spends most of his or her time trying to be an operator rather than a manager. Elements of this may even sometimes be necessary in smaller organisations. Like many other life events – school to work, single to married, childless to parent, volunteer to paid staff –

becoming a manager involves a transition process, and the difficulties in making that adjustment can often be underestimated. Part of that transition is to accept not only that your job is a substantially different one but also to deal with other people's changed expectations of you. You have now acquired the 'manager' label. People will relate to you differently, expecting decisions, answers, action, authority and so on. You should use these expectations to help you to change; after all, people won't expect you to do the same as before, so don't try to. The security of what you know and your behaviours in your past job may be of little use to you in the new role and, as in Don's case, will probably be a handicap.

However, just to complicate life a little we are not saying you can *never* be a player–manager – in fact many voluntary sector managers have to do much hands-on work. We *are* saying that you first need to have the management side of your role under control before you spend much time doing what the operators are doing. And remember to watch whose toes you are treading on when you do join in!

Managerial effectiveness

Most of the discussion in this chapter has focused on the individual manager. You have a collection of uniquely personal knowledge, skills and attitudes that play a part in how effective you are as a manager. Our review of first principles – being amenable to changing ideas about management, improving your communications, being efficient and effective – should enhance your performance. But as well as this personal focus we need to have an overview of some of the other factors and variables that will contribute to how effective you can be. We will raise these in more detail as key issues elsewhere in the book.

Your job

First there is your job. People have expectations from the particular job as well as expecting you to have broader management characteristics. How good the partnership is between the unique you and the unique job you've got will impact directly on your effectiveness. We have discussed to some extent how well you function using the Mintzberg framework (see pages 6–8) and the need to review this. Roles and role theory are discussed in more detail in Chapter 3.

Your colleagues

Next there are the people you work with. Whether they be paid staff or volunteers they can exert a major influence on your effectiveness. A volunteer can undermine your plans for change as easily as a senior manager can overrule you. Our working definition of good management, *getting people to do the right job well*, is clearly a measure of how effective you are. You are in the driving seat when it comes to getting the best out of your team, to communicate well with them, to help them to do the right job and to motivate them to do it well. We look at motivating individuals in more detail in Chapter 5, and helping volunteers to work better in teams in Chapter 6. We also believe that recruitment and selection issues will become increasingly important, and we address those in Chapter 7.

Your organisation

What about the organisation you work for, both at a local level and as a whole entity? Its structure and culture will either constrain you or give you the support you need to be as effective as you can. We looked at this briefly on the helicopter trip and will examine it again in more detail in Chapter 3.

The wider world

Finally, the wider world can significantly influence how effective you can be. Changes in demography and social trends affect your clients; changes in the economy affect people's ability to donate time and money; changes in the law can change the way you do business. We talk about contracting as a topical issue in the voluntary sector in the next chapter, Chapter 2. Another social trend, growing consumerism, will become important to how well you deliver your service and how your organisation is perceived. We explore this in Chapter 8.

We know how difficult it is to keep on top of all this yourself, but as a manager you have to keep volunteers up to speed as well. We believe we can help you with this by polishing a range of your management skills as we proceed through the book.

2 All change

Being associated with the voluntary sector you will appreciate that there is a great deal of change impacting on it. A first principle of effective management is being able to manage yourself and others through change. As Handy says, there is no point in trying to stand still when the ground under your feet is moving.

This chapter reviews some of the major changes currently affecting the sector. Some broad change themes in society are examined briefly to appreciate the changing context. Where appropriate, some historical, legislative or policy background is given. The management of change itself is picked up in Chapter 7.

An analytical tool that managers often find useful to examine change influences is called a STEP analysis. The STEP initials stand for four major groups of change factors – Social or sociological, Technological, Environmental and Political. The nature of the factors influencing most voluntary organisations fall into the social and political groups, and we shall concentrate on these in this chapter. There are, of course, a number of environmental factors which are the *raison d'être* for some charities – for example, Friends of the Earth and many heritage charities. Legislature is one of the largest factors in the political group.

Our changing society

More than twenty years ago Toffler coined the phrase 'futureshock' to describe the state of bewilderment that people find themselves in because of the relentless increase in the pace of change in society (Toffler, 1970). If anything, the pace of change has become faster still and is primarily driven by an explosion in our technical knowledge and its applications.

A century or more ago sociologists began describing the impact on society of a different set of rapid changes or 'revolutions' – the agrarian, industrial, political and intellectual. Tönnies (1855–1936), a German social theorist and philosopher, is generally held to be the founding father of community studies. In his thesis *Community and Association* (1955) he describes two types of societies. The *traditional society* is characterised by a sense of community and a sense of place (social and geographical) and belonging. Common values bond the society together – family loyalties, neighbourliness, enduring relationships and common enemies. Religion, lifestyles and customs are all shared. In contrast *industrial society* is competitive and the population highly mobile. Relationships are not ends in themselves but means to profit and self-interest and are therefore more superficial, impersonal and calculating. Business ethics are the dynamic which replaces the controlling influence of the Church and the family. Other sociologists such as Weber and Durkheim have developed similar theoretical positions. In everyday terms we can say that what we have come to know as the 'rat race' began with the industrial society.

Many more social studies have focused on communities, their strengths, values and so on, often with conflicting outcomes. It is probably safe to assume that the extensive urbanisation which accompanied the Industrial Revolution didn't entirely transport the rural spirit of community into urban life and that here a sense of community is often more fragile. Political commentators would argue that, in the UK, years of the Thatcher government resulted in a more selfish society. Mrs Thatcher herself said, ' There is no such thing as society.'

These apparent changes in society, marked by trends towards insularity, increasing consumerism and competitiveness and fear of involvement are creating real difficulties for voluntary organisations. They may explain some of the difficulty that voluntary organisations have in attracting recruits to provide community services.

At a broad level it is difficult to grasp even a shared definition of such terms as 'society' or 'community', let alone agree how these have changed. Our views are coloured by our own experience, age, background, where we live and so on. For some, the changes seem insidious and, for others, they are quite dramatic. This makes it difficult to stand back and take an objective look at what has changed in the last 50 or even 20 years. Apart from the welfare state, which we shall look at in detail, there have been other significant changes in many other aspects of society. Family structure, size and mobility have all changed. Housing trends have changed. Crime rates and crime patterns have altered. Both education and health care have also seen marked developments. For many, 'work' is now a very different type of experience from that of our parents.

Some of these trends have more of an impact on the work of voluntary organisations than others. One example is that many families now feel that both partners have to work, which causes difficulties when trying to find time to care for elderly relatives. Neither modern housing styles nor today's values encourage younger families to take in an elderly relative. The erosion of welfare support often draws resentment from people who are asked to contribute financially to their own social care needs. In view of these factors, it is appropriate to take a deeper look at the changes in welfare provision and their implications.

The changing welfare state

The meaning of the term 'welfare state' or 'welfare society' has been debated by many. Simply, it could be defined as a society 'in which there is a general recognition of a collective responsibility for the welfare of its more unfortunate members'. Such an attitude is comparatively recent and cannot be effectively present without a democratic framework and a body of ideals held by most members of the society.

Lloyd George is credited with founding the welfare state. The Liberal government passed the Old Age Pension Act in 1908, giving a married couple aged over 70 the right to claim a pension of 7s 6d per week. The 1911 National Insurance Act enabled workers to insure themselves, though not their dependants, for medical attention from a 'panel' doctor. It also gave limited cash payments and medicines. Between the two World Wars national housing and education policies were developed, and the social security system was enhanced for widows and orphans. The retirement age was reduced to 65 years.

Lord Beveridge is held up as the welfare state's modern pioneer. His 1942 committee identified the five giants of Want, Idleness, Disease, Squalor and Ignorance. His proposals led, in 1946, to the passage of the National Health Service Act which became operational on 5 July 1948. In the same year both the National Assistance Act and the Children Act were passed as welfare reforms. The first resulted in local authorities being given responsibilities for the provision of accommodation for homeless people. The second integrated many diverse responsibilities for children's services into one department, to be part of the Department of Health and Social Security (DHSS) from 1971. At the outset local authorities were given the responsibility for care of people with mental health problems in the community. All in all, this was a busy time for them!

The delivery of social services, however, remained fragmented from the recipient's perspective. The Seebohm Report (1968) and the Barclay Report (1980) recommended further changes to social work practice to better fit it to contemporary social need. But, despite an almost continuous programme of post-war legislation and review, the welfare services continued to be severely strained. Some writers have postulated that the original founders of the system never envisaged that the state would have to *continue* to meet the welfare needs of an expanding and ageing population. Their intention was to deliver short-term solutions to Lord Beveridge's five giants, after which we would be a fit and productive society. Certainly, it must have been difficult for them to foresee the consequences of technological developments in medicine, changing social circumstances and the effects of 'boom–bust' national and world economies in recent years.

Ken Young, Professor of Politics at London University argues that the Beveridge compact has been overwhelmed by three forces: the loss of society's homogeneity; an explosion in the number and variety of special needs and claims; and an expansion in citizen's views about their entitlements or social rights considerably beyond what Beveridge envisaged (cited in Lloyd, 1993).

Recent trends, which are predicted to continue and which will have implicit welfare consequences, include:

1 *The closure of all large long-stay hospital institutions.* All those people with mental health problems and learning disabilities currently in institutions are likely to have their care provided in community settings. All long-stay institutions are likely to be closed by 2002. Many more dependent people will need care in community settings, part of which will be delivered by voluntary organisations.
2 *The 'rising tide' of elderly people.* The most significant increase will be in the over-75s with their related associated social and medical needs. The projected increase is from 3.6 million aged 75 and over in 1991 to 4 million by 2001 (Carey, 1993). One million of these people will be 85 plus; many will be increasingly dependent and will live alone. Meeting their social care needs will require considerable human resources..

Other trends include:

- the tendency to care for the young chronic sick in the community as opposed to giving residential hospital care
- the increased numbers of those receiving palliative and terminal care in the community, including those with HIV and AIDS
- increasing numbers of people with drug and alcohol related problems
- increasing competition for young workers, the traditional source of recruits (often referred to as the 'demographic timebomb').

Against this backdrop of developing trends you can see why an examination of the voluntary sector contribution to community care is high on the agenda for all political parties.

The community care agenda

What is community care?

Community care is another 'difficult to define' concept. It is typically used to refer to care given within the client's own home or to a range of community-based services, whether residential, day care or domiciliary support, which prevent or forestall the need for admission to residential care, or provide a real alternative to institutional care.

Probably the best starting point is the Department of Health and Social Security's 1981 statement:

> Strengthened primary and community care services will help elderly people to live independently in their own homes; services for those who are mentally ill, including in some cases residential, day care and other support will enable them to keep in touch with their normal lives, and services for mentally handicapped people will enable them to live with their families, or failing that in a supportive local community setting. Such services require the co-operation of neighbourhood and voluntary support, primary health care and personal social services. (DHSS, 1981)

The government White Paper, *Caring for People: Community Care in the Next Decade and Beyond* (DoH, 1989), defines community care as:

> Providing the services and support which people who are affected by problems of ageing, mental illness, mental handicap or physical or sensory disability need to be able to live as independently as possible in their own homes, or in 'homely' settings in the community. (Ch. 1, para. 1.1)

The report goes on to say:

> Community Care means providing the right level of intervention and support to enable people to achieve maximum independence and control over their own lives. For this aim to become a reality, the development of a wide range of services provided in a variety of settings is essential. These services form part of a spectrum of care ranging from domiciliary support provided to people in their own homes, strengthened by the availability of respite care and day care for those with more intensive needs, through sheltered residential care and nursing homes and long stay hospital care for those for whom other forms of care are no longer enough. (Ch. 2, para. 2.2)

Kathleen Jones, Professor of Social Policy at the University of York, more succinctly captures different interpretations of community care in the following passage:

To the politician, community care is a useful piece of rhetoric: to the sociologist it is a stick to beat institutional care with: To the civil servant it is a cheap alternative to institutional care which can be passed to the local authorities for action or inaction: To the visionary, it is a dream of the new society in which people really do care: To social services departments, it is a nightmare of heightened public expectation and inadequate resources to meet them. (Jones, Brown and Bradshaw, 1978:114)

The theory is easier to describe than the practice. Who will actually do what? What will be statutory and what voluntary? What will be health and what will be social care? How will agencies work together? Does community care mean just 'care within the community' or a fuller notion of 'care *by* the community'? With regard to this last question does community care simply mean care by specialist staff within purpose-built accommodation – 'an institution within the community' – or does it imply people leading as normal a lifestyle as is possible, supported by the local people with the aid of specialist services as appropriate? Walker suggests that community care will be provided by 'informal, quasi-formal, or formal helpers, or by a combination of all three' (1982:3).

Implementing community care: issues for voluntary organisations

The implications for voluntary organisations are that they clearly have to make their own decisions about their own purposes and how they will deliver these. Just as there is a spectrum of care there is a spectrum of funding sources. Voluntary organisations may decide they can best meet their remit from contract funding, through grants or trying to remain independent.

The pros and cons of these decisions are discussed below under 'The contract culture' (pages 22–25) but the resourcing implications challenge both the government and voluntary sector alike. Government spending on elderly health and social services rose by an average 3.4 per cent per year in real terms from 1979–80 to 1989–90 (DoH, 1993). The government will clearly be concerned to manage this expenditure, and there is already an element of it in subcontracting welfare provision to charitable agencies. The Charities Aid Foundation showed that funding of voluntary bodies had grown 21 per cent from 1989–90 to 1993–94, and data from the NCVO suggests that much of this is for contract or agreement-based fees which rose 154 per cent between 1990–91 and 1993–94. Total annual donations from private and corporate sources of £17 billion have stagnated since about 1988.

The National Health Service and Community Care Act 1990

The implementation of community care is likely to be the largest single issue affecting voluntary organisations working in this field over the next few years. We shall explore three strategic aspects to its implementation, which voluntary organisation managers need to understand fully: an appreciation of the NHS and Community Care Act 1990; the impact of the Citizen's Charter; and, finally, the contract culture.

The NHS and Community Care Act 1990 was preceded by at least 11 different government-sponsored reports examining the provision of care in the community in the previous decade. The most significant were:

- The Audit Commission Report (1988), *Making a Reality of Community Care*
- The Wagner Report (1987), *Residential Care and Positive Choice*
- The Griffiths Report (1988), *Community Care: an Agenda for Action*
- The NHS White Paper (1989), *Working for Patients*
- The NHS White Paper (1989), *Caring for People: Community Care in the Next Decade and Beyond*

The NHS and Community Care Act became law in June 1990 with gradual implementation up until April 1993. It encompassed many of the recommendations made in preceding reports in recognition of the changes within society, health and social care.

The key objectives of the Act are:

- to promote and develop domiciliary, day and respite care services to enable people to live in their own homes wherever feasible and sensible
- to ensure that service providers make practical support for carers a high priority
- to make assessment of need and good case management the cornerstone of high quality care
- to promote the development of a flourishing independent sector alongside good quality public services
- to clarify the responsibilities of agencies and so make it easier to hold them accountable for their performance
- to secure better value for taxpayers' money by introducing a new funding structure for community care.

From the voluntary sector's perspective the fourth of these objectives is the most important. The Act encourages a 'mixed economy' of care, requiring local authorities to involve private and voluntary care agencies. There is an implicit requirement to ensure that value for money is balanced against the quality of service. Ideally, the best possible service should be delivered at the most cost-effective price. The Act also recognises the historic and contemporary contribution of individual volunteers and volunteer groups to the maintainance of people requiring care in the community. It encourages local authorities to work even more closely with voluntary organisations in the provision of quality community services. The means to do this will be by entering into contracts or service agreements for providing care.

Under the Act local authorities are required to prepare and publish Community Care Plans in consultation with the principal providers of care services, service users and their carers. These should detail the proposed provision of services to the community. Voluntary organisations should be locally consulted in this process. As a voluntary sector manager you should be able to identify the key person, within your local social services structure, responsible for liaison with volunteers. If you don't know who it is you can enquire through your organisation or establish contact through your local social service office.

In practice the formal procedure for providing community care to an individual is as below. This procedure enables voluntary organisations and volunteers themselves to contribute at three key points. You may *refer* to social services someone who you think needs help. You may be asked to *contribute information to an assessment* of someone to whom you have been providing services. You may be asked if you can *provide an aspect of care*, either on a purely voluntary basis or as part of grant-funded or contracted activity.

- **The initial request.** This is made by the individual or by a third party. Social services will seek to obtain as much information as possible about the individual needing help. This may involve asking other agencies, including volunteers.
- **Screening.** A decision will be made as to the need for assessment, based on the information provided. The vulnerability of the individual concerned will be taken into consideration.
- **Assessment.** Assessments are used to decide whether an individual needs care, meets criteria for eligibility and also whether they will have to contribute financially (means testing). A key worker will manage and coordinate the assessments. Joint assessment between health and social care will be undertaken where necessary. The client and carers will be encouraged to fully participate in this process.
- **Care planning.** This is the process where options for meeting the individual's needs are discussed. Costing implications will arise in respect of the service costs and the client's ability to contribute.
- **Care purchasing.** Clients will be offered choices where available and advised about organisations that can meet their needs. This may include voluntary sector provision.

- **Service provision.** Organisations that provide care will have to be involved in identifying how best the assessed needs may be met by their organisation. Service providers will be monitored for continuing quality of service.
- **Service provision review.** There should follow a review after a period of service delivery to ensure that care remains appropriate.

The Citizen's Charter

The Citizen's Charter, first introduced in 1991, has been an important government policy initiative in moving the rights of the consumer to centre stage. The initiative covers a wide range of services offered by public bodies including the National Health Service, public utilities such as gas and electricity, the Inland Revenue and the emergency services – police, fire and ambulance. From 1 April 1996 local councils will have to produce Community Care Charters and should have involved voluntary organisations in their production. Voluntary organisations and their volunteers are likely to be bound by the emerging standards if they are contracting with social services.

One of the largest areas of charter development to date has been the Patient's Charter, which sets out our rights and expectations as consumers of the National Health Service. Experience so far may signal what the voluntary sector can expect over the next few years. In the Patient's Charter the government sets national standards of service and requires health purchasing authorities to deliver on these and to additionally set its own local standards.

The desired impact of the Charter movement is to empower people through making them more aware of the standards of service they should expect and to give them the right of challenge when they do not receive expected standards of care. Voluntary organisations will not be immune to this general raising of consumer expectations. We should be actively considering our responses to the Charter environment, particularly in respect of our operating standards and the rights of our customers to complain should we fail to meet their expectations.

We have met managers in some large voluntary organisations who behave rather like King Canute in this area of user empowerment. Some argue against the introduction of a complaints system for service users. It may be that change in itself is threatening, but we have found examples where the service is barely adequate. Their conflict is that they believe that people receiving services from volunteers should not complain. Yet those people may be paying for that service and, in today's developing consumer culture, it will become an untenable stance not to offer a responsive service. We will explore this issue further in Chapter 4.

Organisations offering public services are eligible to apply for a

Chartermark award in recognition of the excellence of the quality of the services they deliver.

The contract culture

Obtaining adequate finance for voluntary organisation activities is becoming increasingly challenging. The NHS and Community Care Act signalled both an end to the days when voluntary organisations received grants from local authorities as of right and a consequent expansion in contract-based services. The 'contract culture' is a simple means of describing the new way voluntary organisations will have to do business with statutory organisations.

Total donations to charities from individuals have declined over recent years although the level of corporate donations is being maintained. However, total donations are being spread wider because of the growing numbers of voluntary groups. The effects of the National Lottery on direct giving and the proportion shared out to charities have yet to be worked through, although the picture is becoming clearer. An NCVO survey at the end of 1994 estimated that the lottery could divert 4 per cent of charities' income. The fact that Tenovus, a leading cancer charity, scrapped its long-running scratch card game, with the loss of 500 jobs, in March 1995 after a 25 per cent decline in income is evidence that there will be winners and losers. A joint survey carried out by the *Community Care* magazine and the NCVO in February 1995 showed that two-thirds of their sample of 60 national charities contracted with local authorities or other agencies and suggested an increased tendency for charities to engage in direct service provision. The proportion of their income from contracted activity ranges from 4–100 per cent.

The contract environment is causing voluntary organisations to take stock of their predicament, especially in a financial sense. It takes a while to weigh up its pros and cons. In a positive light, and one which you can share with volunteers, is the fact that some contractors will recognise your strengths.

- You may have more local knowledge, experience and expertise.
- You better understand user perspectives.
- 'Voluntary' does not mean amateur or cheap.
- Your independence can be an asset.

You should be able to market these assets but, at the same time, need to convince contractors that they need to make a commitment to you because:

- most improvements will come from funding long-term relationships
- training and development has a cost
- small-size contracts and tailored services also cost a little extra.

At the worst extreme you may have the misfortune to be approached by a contractor who:

- excludes you from any planning input
- is exclusively price-driven
- underestimates, or fails to appreciate, your costs
- doesn't recognise your professionalism or competence or their responsibility or the sense in supporting a thriving voluntary sector.

There are clearly different reactions to the contract culture on both sides and it will take a few years for this to work through. Naomi Eisenstadt, Assistant Director of NCVO, feels that part of the problem is that local authorities have little freedom to act. There is nothing wrong in local government or the NHS seeking to place contracts with voluntary groups, but the process itself can strangle innovation, discriminate against smaller charities and constrain the larger ones. Richard Gutch, Chief Executive of Arthritis Care, has taken a policy decision not to get involved in contracting. He believes that the time and money spent in contract negotiations can hamper one's ability to raise voluntary income because less time is available for raising one's campaigning profile. Furthermore, if a voluntary organisation becomes a major service provider dependent on a local authority contract, it restricts its ability to act as a pressure group.

If you haven't any personal involvement with contracting here are some examples of ways in which you may become involved:

- seeking continuation of funding for a service which you already provide – for example, a luncheon club for older people or operating a youth organisation
- responding to a competitive tender request from the local authority
- being directly approached by the local authority to provide a service.

Competitive tendering in particular is a complex task, and you may want to seek further advice. Many larger voluntary organisations and social service training departments offer support courses.

Should you become involved in making any tender bid or responding to a contract enquiry the contractor will expect you to demonstrate your fitness to manage the contract. You should be prepared to offer the information in the checklist below.

Checklist: Are you fit for a contract?

Can you supply the following:

- evidence that there is a need for the service, based preferably on research?
- a clear mission statement about your organisation, including its value base, and its objectives?
- details of the organisation's resource base – financial, human and collateral?
- details of your management structure including support and training systems, with particular emphasis on how they will fit in to the project?
- a volunteering policy, setting out your expectations of volunteers, grievance procedures and so on?
- adherence to relevant legislation – for example, a copy of your Health and Safety Policy, Food Handling Standards, Fire Regulations and so on?
- adequate insurance cover for the purpose?
- an equal opportunities policy covering both your volunteers and your customers?
- a consultation and complaints system for users?
- evidence that you operate a quality assurance system?
- an explanation of how you will continue to communicate with and report to the funding agency during the lifetime of the project?
- a business plan detailing how you intend operating the service over a set time frame?

Note the issues that will have a particular bearing on the management of volunteers, such as your values, human resources, training, a volunteer policy, equal opportunities, a complaints management system and so on. To offer a specific example of tendering for a contract to offer a respite care service you would additionally need to include:

- pump-priming or set-up costs (telephone answering machine, initial mileage costs and so on)
- resources available
- time limits
- client group to be served
- training of volunteers, curriculum, trainers, costs of training
- management and support systems including monitoring of quality
- a timetable of service development and expansion
- a projection of services costs

● details of the amount of grant aid you are seeking.

Some managers may feel that this all looks very bureaucratic and daunting. We have attempted to give some reassurance that sound local authorities want and need to work closely with voluntary organisations. In our experience agencies are prepared to guide and work alongside voluntary groups seeking to enter into a contract or service agreement with them, providing that the service is demonstrably required and the supplier organisation can demonstrate the quality and reliability of its services.

There is concern that competition may have an adverse effect on some organisations, perhaps smaller ones being absorbed by the larger national societies. However, our experience is that there is a commitment to the small local organisation. Generally one voluntary organisation will not seek to undermine the activity of another already operating the service in a geographical area. Indeed, it will seek to consult with specialist organisations prior to embarking on any project within their remit.

We predict that, as a result of reduced resources, voluntary agencies will increasingly jointly plan and operate projects. This pooling of resources, whether financial or in terms of volunteers themselves, may not only achieve the care objective but lead us into a new era of partnership where we put client or community needs above those of our individual organisation.

3 Volunteers and the organisation

Purpose, mission, vision, values and all that

One thing people find irritating about management is the jargon. It is no different to any other specialism in that it has its own language, created to help the experts talk to each other in a shorthand way. The title of this section contains a number of popular buzzwords which broadly concern 'what we're all doing and why'. We can only understand how to manage ourselves and our volunteers effectively in the context of some clear direction in which we're all heading in. We'll translate as we go along.

Purpose

One crucial message we need to convey in this chapter is that people in organisations (preferably all of them) should know some key facts about their organisation. We're not talking about the day-to-day facts such as where you sit, when pay-day is, where to get coffee and biscuits and so on but, first and foremost, what your organisation's purpose is. Do you know what your organisation is supposed to be doing? Why is it in existence? Who for? Who is it supposed to benefit?

In our experience not everyone is sure about the answers to these seem-ingly obvious questions. That doesn't help if you're a manager, since man-agers are supposed to be using staff, often volunteers, to deliver the organisation's purpose. All organisations exist for a purpose, or at least they came into existence for a purpose. You should be clear about why your organisation came into existence and whether it is trying to fulfil the same purpose now.

Organisations are groups of two or more people working together to fulfil a need, either of their own or of somebody else. If they are to primarily serve their own or members' interests they might be termed as a 'club' or 'society' or even 'union', or be a professional body. However, more commonly when we refer to organisations we mean the trading organisations participating in the market to offer products or services. Often starting as small, or even one-person, concerns they may serve the owner's or shareholders' interests primarily by offering products or services to customers. As such, the work-force must focus on the interests of others, often called stakeholders. Increasingly customer's interests are becoming a driving force here. Arguably, the major differences between private and public sector organisa-tions are related to (a) the extent to which the organisation has to compete to survive or has a protected position with guaranteed funding, or (b) the extent to which the service provided has been viewed as a core service for society from a political or ideological perspective. Recent political direction has introduced more private sector provision into social care and created an 'internal' market in the NHS.

So, what of the voluntary sector? Usually voluntary organisations have come into being to serve the interests of particular groups of people with par-ticular needs which are often not met or are poorly provided for by existing arrangements. Voluntary organisations fulfil one or more of three purposes:

- to provide specific services
- to provide information or research
- to raise awareness, often by acting in an advocacy capacity.

Example: Purpose – The Compassionate Friends

A voluntary organisation called The Compassionate Friends was founded in 1969 when Reverend Simon Stephens introduced two couples newly bereaved of their child to each other. He witnessed the therapeutic value of their resulting friendship. In the organisation's leaflet it states:

> The original aim of The Compassionate Friends was to be a self-help group of bereaved parents offering friendship and understanding to each other and this will remain its primary purpose.

This statement makes the organisation's purpose clear and explicit; it is pri-marily to give a service of friendship to bereaved parents.

Since your organisation was founded its purpose may have changed some-what in response to society's changing needs and circumstances. An obvious example of this is the Order of St John. Originally founded in the twelfth century it was principally a military religious order defending the Holy Land. Its role faded with the decline of the Turkish empire in the eighteenth century. In search of a new role its English members founded the St John Ambulance Association in 1877 to provide instruction on first aid and ambulance transport to the public, at home and at work. The Association is now the country's leading supplier of first aid training. The St John Ambulance Brigade was founded in 1887 to support public events with ambulance transport and volunteers trained in first aid.

We emphasize the point because it is not only important for you, as a manager, to know about your organisation's purpose but also to be aware of the changing contexts in which you and the organisation operate. Nowadays, St John volunteers do not join to fight a Holy War nor does that aspect of the Association's past have any particular relevance to its current function (although it still supports an ophthalmic hospital in Jerusalem).

Let's take a favourite, if lighthearted, analogy – a football team. A football team is an organisation. What is its purpose? Well, it's simple, you might say – to win the game by getting the ball in the net at the other end more times than the opposition gets it in your net. Is that a wholly safe assumption? Some players might just want to enjoy the game, or get some exercise, or escape from other commitments, or keep up with the lads, or enjoy the mud or whatever. They may not care who wins, or may not need to win as much as you do. Just because everybody is on the same side doesn't guarantee that they all share the same purpose! Ensuring that they do is the job of the skillful manager. Examining your understanding of your organisation's purpose will help you start to analyse how well you are managing.

Exercise 3.1   Your organisation's purpose

Try to define, in writing, what you think your organisation's purpose is, using just a few clear and unambiguous sentences. Is there any printed example of its purpose that you can refer to?

Mission

Organisations often try to remind themselves and the rest of the world what their purpose is. Senior management also has to try injecting purpose into its workforce. One way of doing this is using the mission approach, often written down as a mission statement which is essentially a dynamic way of sharing your organisation's purpose for the benefit of workers and customers alike. You can probably imagine the football team coach reminding the team of the mission in the dressing room at the start of the match: 'We're here to win.' You can also imagine the coach questioning the team's purpose at half-time when they come in losing by two goals: 'What the bloody hell do you think you are doing out there?'

The analogy could well be extended to examine teamwork, by asking if everybody thinks they're on the same side, playing the same game, on the same pitch and so on. You might well ask some of these questions in your own organisation at times!

Example: Mission statement – Elizabeth Fitzroy Homes

'Our Mission is to provide support, dignity, opportunity and individual choice to those of all ages with a profound learning disability and to encourage their continued development in a normal and caring environment, where appropriate for life.'

Vision

Another strategy that helps to focus people in your organisation is to try to create a vision for the organisation. A vision is a picture of the kinds of activities your organisation will be carrying out – for example, the way it provides services. Do you know what your organisation aspires to be like in three or five years' time? Having some idea of the organisation's perceived destination clearly helps with the journey. If you can't sketch out the picture for the workforce how can you guide their efforts towards the purpose?

We will illustrate this with the following exercise.

Exercise 3.2   What is success in your organisation?

Describe in a couple of sentences how you see success in your organisation or your department.

You might have completed the above exercise easily or you might have thought that it was particularly vague. Did you describe what you'd like to see people doing or the results you would want to see? Were you able to use any images to make your picture of success more vivid? Could you share these with volunteers? If you found the exercise vague you should ask yourself how you will know when success has arrived. You need to have a fairly clear picture of how it would be when your organisation had fulfilled its purpose.

The professional football manager's vision would probably have the word 'Cup' in it somewhere and be further coloured by some of the rewards that success would bring. Our vision in writing this book is that some managers will make great use of it, they'll recommend it to others who'll also buy it, it will help them deal with some of their issues more effectively, and in a year or so the publisher will come back to us to write a second edition. The vision of an environmental charity may be to stop all nuclear testing worldwide, a heritage charity may have saved and restored a particular listed building and so on.

Does your organisation have a vision? Do you have one for your part of the organisation? Can you describe to your staff where you're trying to get to? If not, have a go at describing one. You should find it easier than before. The question now is: can you share it with the people you work with?

Values

Before we discuss values try the exercise below.

Exercise 3.3   Clarifying values

Imagine yourself in the following scenario:

You work for a charity that offers help to elderly people. You ask a volunteer to go and visit a refugee family which has been placed in a council house by social services. You are aware that the family comprises an elderly gentleman with some mobility problems, his son and his wife and young baby. You offer a vision to the volunteer that the family unit might find it helpful if the elderly gentlemen could visit a lunch club once a week that your organisation runs. The elderly gentleman might find a few new friends and the young family might benefit from some time together. The volunteer's role might be to sound the family out and, if they agree, arrange some volunteer transport.

The volunteer says that she doesn't want to go, that she thought the organisation was supposed to help long-term resident elderly nationals, not refugees, and that's why people give donations.

You thought you had a valid purpose and were helping her by giving her a vision of what you hoped would be achieved. Is she disagreeing with you because of her interpretation of the organisation's values or is she disguising her own values? How will you know?

Clarifying the values of the organisation with her will help. Asking her whether she agrees or not will help. She will have to rethink her position. But what if you're not sure yourself?

This simple exercise about sharing a vision with a volunteer and asking for views is called a value clarification exercise. In it you found out something about the volunteer's values and beliefs which may be at odds with those of the organisation. Values are the set of beliefs the organisation holds dear. They may cover the way in which you work, the context in which you try to achieve your purpose and the outcomes you hope for. Talking about values helps to clarify for those who work for you the expectations you have of them.

To return to the game of football, or almost any other competitive sport, values have changed over time. The game has become more commercialised and competitive; some might say standards of player's conduct have slipped, more aggression is expected and success is celebrated much more overtly. The values volunteers hold will equally have been influenced by many social forces and, in just the same way and for the same reasons that your organisation might declare its mission, they might choose to make statements about its values. You would at least expect volunteers not to be espousing contradictory values whilst carrying out the organisation's business.

Example: Values – The Shaftesbury Society

The Shaftesbury Society celebrated 150 years of Christian care in action in 1993. It was founded in 1843 when the Seventh Earl of Shaftesbury responded to an appeal for help in *The Times* from a struggling Ragged School. The Society's purpose is 'to enable people in great need to achieve security, self-worth and significance'. This purpose is underpinned by their values of demonstrating Christian care in action. In its 150th year it set itself the task of calling Britain's churches to social action. An extract from Lord Shaftesbury's diary said: 'I was convinced that God had called me to devote whatever advantages He might have bestowed upon me in the cause of the weak, the helpless . . . and those who had none to help them.'

One reason why values and beliefs are important is that those held by senior managers influence the way everything is done in the organisation. Mostly these values are well synchronised with its purpose but sometimes they can be 'out of step'. The choice of a military metaphor is quite deliberate. The origins of older voluntary organisations are likely to be tied closely to one or more of three 'traditions': military, religious/vocational or paternalistic. These traditional mindsets are likely to have had several sorts of influences on the way an organisation structures itself, the backgrounds of the volunteers it attracts and the values that can come packaged with the services it offers.

'So what?' you might say. You might rightly be proud of the traditions of your organisation. But one of the questions these issues raise concerns the match between what your purpose is, or should be, and whether the values that influence such factors as your structure or recruitment actually help or hinder you in delivering your purpose.

Strong Christian traditions are likely to influence management style in an organisation like the Shaftesbury Society. A different set of underlying organisational values will influence management approaches in the British Legion. During 1994 the British Legion adopted a new softer logo in trying to shed its 'world war' image of benefiting only veterans. It was trying to modernise its values. It reiterated its mission as set out in its Royal Charter, to help the needy in the ex-service community.

Organisational cultures

What we have been discussing in the last few paragraphs is *organisational culture* – the 'way things are done' in organisations as determined by the beliefs and values of those that lead them and strongly coloured by their heritage. Traditional views about the structure of organisations are that they should be quite hierarchical, with several layers from top to bottom, with chains of command, with fairly narrow spans of control and so on. There is a degree of military heritage here and a persisting view that 'if it works well for them then it will do for us'.

More recently many organisations have been shedding layers of management, giving more autonomy to individuals and teams, widening and loosening spans of control and encouraging self-organising teams. Newer ways of organising can seem quite alien to some managers and older volunteers who may be seeking the certainty of functional departments, organisational charts and fixed job descriptions. Helping volunteers to integrate themselves into this change of values will be one of the voluntary sector manager's future challenges.

You might also consider the client's perspective. In general it is reasonable to say that the elderly are used to services being fairly paternalistic. Often they do not want to question the judgement or standard of services given and adopt a trusting and 'you know best' attitude. The notions of institutionalisation and learned helplessness are well documented in the caring professions. The risks here are that volunteers or their managers may create client dependency on services by the values they hold about how services should be given. Younger clients may experience difficulties with being offered help with certain values attached. Again, managers need to be alert to potential conflicts between the values of their organisation and of the volunteers working for it.

There are no easy solutions to any of the dilemmas raised by these issues. We have already pointed out many of the existing conflicts and the benefit of continual dialogue with volunteers about purpose, structure and values. Successful organisations now try to use the management approach known as *contingency theory* – an attempt to find the 'best fit' between their organisation and all these potentially conflicting issues. Our earlier example, the British Legion adopted this approach in trying to achieve a more contemporary fit with current needs.

Exercise 3.4   Contingency theory and your department

Consider these questions about your department:

- Are you employing the best way of organising your department's work given the task, the range of people involved, the purpose of the organisation and the demands of your clients?
- How explicit are your statements of purpose, mission, values and so on to your volunteers?
- What changes might you reasonably make and expect others to make?
- How can you make those changes?
- How will you keep everybody motivated?

These are fairly demanding questions, many of which will be tackled later in the book. Some we will address by examining your role in the organisation and how it comes to be defined. We will tackle this issue now.

Your role in the organisation

In most organisations, of any size, there is some sort of organising principle causing groupings or division of labour. It might be functional – for example, marketing, research, fundraising – but, more commonly in voluntary organisations, it will be geographical – for example, head office, branch or area offices. Whatever the principle your management task will be made easier if you are as clear as possible about your role.

Like many other management ideas, role theory can seem nebulous. You will recognise that you already have a number of 'roles' in life. Some you might be entirely happy with, others less so; some may be foisted on you, others you may choose. Dressmaker or gardener may be roles you choose and enjoy, whereas scapegoat is neither chosen nor pleasant. Roles like parent and manager can demand some self-adjustment.

Roles in organisations can be narrowly defined by 'what's in my job description', but are perhaps better defined by the collection of expectations held by those in working relationships with you. Whilst many of these are given there is often some leeway to shape your role in the way you best perceive it.

The previous discussion on purpose obviously has relevance here. One of a manager's principal roles or expectations is to accurately interpret the organisation's purpose into forms of action for him or herself and their team. Parts of organisations have a tendency to take on a life of their own and give rise to conflicting interests between one part and another. This can lead to what is often called 'turf wars' – fighting for territory within an organisation rather than working collaboratively to achieve its purpose.

Role expectations

Being clear about your role means being clear about what you think your manager expects of you. If you are unsure you should clarify this. You may do this in several ways: in consultation with your manager; by reference to your job description (if you have one that you feel is still up-to-date); or by reference to Exercise 3.5 below. You may have heard the saying 'What interests my manager fascinates me'. Later, in Chapter 6, we shall tackle such issues as setting objectives as a means of delivering your manager's expectations.

Volunteers also need to be clear about your role. Not only will you have expectations of them but they will have expectations of you. You should keep them informed of your changing expectations of them, and you may need to help them clarify their expectations of you.

Role clarification

Some organisations have role clarification built into their traditions by having recognisable role signs – uniforms, badges, epaulettes, hats, pips and so on.

Clarifying your role is an important exercise. It will help to avoid:

- *role ambiguity* – not being sure what your role is, or being undecided between two or more alternatives
- *role conflict* – where one expectation of you is in opposition to another expectation of you
- *role overload* – where you are being expected to perform too many roles, often simultaneously.

You will have no trouble in recognising the importance of resolving these role issues if any of them apply to you. But how do you clarify roles for the volunteers you work with?

Exercise 3.5   Role clarification for yourself or volunteers

Ask yourself the following questions or choose two or three volunteers to discuss them with.

To check for role ambiguity:

- How clear are you about your role?
- Is any aspect of what is expected of you confusing to you?

To check for role conflict:

- Does anything that you are expected to do conflict with anything else that is expected of you?
- Are you being pulled in more than one direction by managers or staff?

To check for role overload:

- Do you think your manager expects you to do too much/too many things at once?

You might feel quite comfortable about the above questions or you may already be aware that you are postponing some issues. Managing some of the issues that may arise could be quite difficult and involve you in a chain of events with other volunteers, other managers or directly with clients. However, as you probably already realise, volunteers will welcome and respect you for trying to help with the problems that confront them, and the next three chapters will discuss many approaches to managing yourself and managing and supporting individual staff and volunteers.

4 Managing yourself effectively

This chapter and the two which follow are based on the premise that to manage well requires good self-knowledge. Although there are many other competences to management, the ability to analyse your strengths and weaknesses is fundamental to success. Here we discuss the importance of setting boundaries around your limitations and the key personal skills needed in self-management – managing stress and time, delegation and assertiveness.

Knowing your strengths and weaknesses

Whatever your career you should ask yourself frequently how well you are doing. Self-confidence is important, especially when things don't seem to be going well since that is when we tend to seek explanations externally rather than from within ourselves. While we may not actually blame others we find external reasons to excuse ourselves from fault: 'It's the way things are in this place' or 'People don't work well together here' and so on.

Knowing as much as possible about yourself means asking yourself and others about how you've managed things – and listening to the answers. The box in Exercise 4.1 below is based on the Johari window, a counselling tool. It will help you to start thinking about what you and others know about you as a manager, and give you a clearer picture of your strengths and weaknesses.

We cannot overstate the importance of regular reflection on your performance. It is not something to be defensive about. Development as a manager is a process of constant self-examination, which means always asking yourself questions about yourself, and dealing with what you find. Of course, not all managers excel at everything nor are they universally poor at their jobs. But some do not learn as much as they might from their management experiences. What was it about how you handled something that made it go well or not so well? How could you do it differently next time? Regularly asking

Exercise 4.1   What do you and others know about you as a manager?

A.
What do I know about myself as a manager that others also know?
e.g. *I always let meetings overrun.*
    Who I used to work for?
    I arrive at work punctually.
	B.
	What do others know about me as a manager that I don't know?
	e.g. *Maybe I appear rude or uncaring.*
	    I may demonstrate favouritism towards certain volunteers.
	    They may know my prejudices better than I do.

C.
What do I know about myself as a manager that those I work with don't know?
e.g. *I'm not very confident about money.*
    I feel stressed about trying to achieve all this with the team I've got.
    I don't like this organisation much.
	D.
	What don't I know that no one else knows either?
	e.g. *How I'll respond during a major crisis.*

Do this exercise for yourself, bearing in mind that it's unlikely you can add to box D. Try to identify at least one strength and one weakness for each of boxes A, B and C. Discuss the questions in box B with someone you trust. Recognising and owning your weaknesses is an important first step in eliminating them.

---

yourself questions like these will help you to improve your management skills.

The importance of knowing your strengths and weaknesses is twofold. First, you can develop those aspects where you recognise shortfalls and therefore become a more 'balanced' and successful manager. Second, you should be aware of those management tasks which you find a real problem so that you can either get help with them, decline them or delegate them. Later in this chapter we will explore some key personal skills such as delegating, managing stress and managing time but first we're going to invite you to do two more exercises that will help this self-exploratory process.

The first is based on a theory by Blake and Mouton (1964) about types of management which, although thirty years old, is still relevant. These authors believed that managers were more likely to be effective when they struck the right balance between 'concern for people' and 'concern for production' or, in today's terms, between being people-focused and task-focused. They tried to plot managerial styles onto a grid which we have adapted below.

Exercise 4.2   Your approach to management

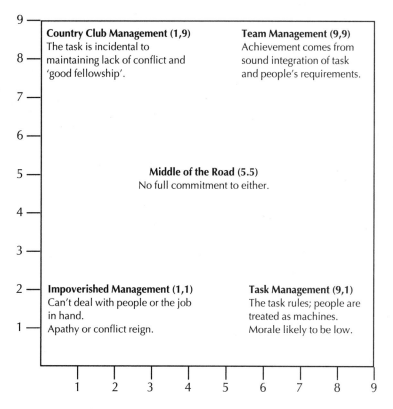

Simply the grid shows that good managers should seek to balance a strong commitment to both people and the management task. There will, of course, be times when a focus on one is more imperative than another, such as meeting a deadline (task) or managing staff sickness (person). Can you recognise your management style from this grid? Do you think those you work with will recognise you? What do you think volunteers in general need?

If the way volunteers are managed in your organisation is in the Blake and Mouton impoverished style or your skills are middle-of-the-road, then clearly you need to develop your management skills further. This book will help with both task and people management skills. Knowing the direction in which you need to develop them may be influenced by a further examination of Mintzberg's ten key roles of management which we first discussed in Chapter 1 (page 6). You could use these roles as a self-appraisal checklist or a management skills inventory as in Exercise 4.3 below.

Exercise 4.3   Management Skills Inventory (after Mintzberg)

Work through the inventory below using the following method:

1   Add any questions of your own which you consider relevant to yourself or your situation.
2   Think about why you haven't answered 'yes' to some questions and what you can do about the reasons for this.
3   Consider each question in particular relation to the volunteers you work with and the implications for both you and them.

Roles	Yes	Working on it	No
Interpersonal			
Figurehead Do I pay enough attention to social or symbolic duties?			
Leader Have I set objectives for each of my team? Do I know what each of my team seeks from the job?			
Liaison What links have I got with other managers in my organisation and other relevant ones? Are these links as helpful as they could be?			

Roles	Yes	Working on it	No
Informational			
Monitor Am I keeping sufficiently in touch with what is going on both within and outside my organisation?			
Disseminator Do I share enough organisation with my team to help them do their job well?			
Spokesperson Do I publicise appropriate information about my organisation? Is it accurate?			
Decisional			
Entrepreneur Do I seek out good ideas or opportunities to improve what my team or organisation is doing?			
Disturbance-handler How well do I manage the unexpected developments?			
Resource-allocator Has each of my team got the right resources to do their job?			
Negotiator How successful am I at negotiating for my team, organisation?			

Well, how did you do at this? To be 'balanced' you ought to be able to answer 'yes' or at least 'working on it' to most of the questions. You may have identified a couple of gaps or areas where you would like to improve. Previous sections of this book should have been helpful, but the next few chapters should be even more so.

Setting boundaries

Setting boundaries is about applying your knowledge of your abilities to work situations so that, where possible, you don't become involved with activities for which you don't possess the skills. This process needs to be extended to setting boundaries around the skills of other team members, whether volunteers or employees. As a manager you will tend to agree to all manner of requests, particularly those from people of influence! It benefits no one if you make a hash of some of these, to say nothing of the stressful effects of failing. The processes of setting boundaries around what you do is not simply just a matter of saying 'Yes, OK, I'll do that' or 'No, that's not my job'. You need to consider both what it might be reasonable for others to expect of you, given who they are and your own role in the organisation, and whether there are situations where your boundary or sphere of influence doesn't extend far enough.

Recognise that you have boundaries in three dimensions – with *superiors*, with your *peers* and with your *staff* – and that these boundaries aren't always fixed. To set boundaries you might use different approaches with each of these categories of people. You might use delegation with staff working for you, assertiveness with your peers and an appeal to reason with your superiors! We cover the first two approaches in this chapter in addition to managing resources, managing stress and managing time – all skills helpful to both developing good relations with others and managing within your limitations. In Chapter 5 we will also address negotiating skills.

Your needs and your resources

Here we look at some of the issues that preoccupy many managers – having the tools to do the job. If you have some management experience you will recognise, however, that merely having the tools isn't always the answer. Quite simply, some people can achieve more with less; others achieve less with more. When faced with any task or project you might ask yourself not just whether you have what you need, but also whether you are making the best use of what you have and what you can do about the resource gap.

Clearly, to achieve anything of consequence you are going to need resources – the right mix of people with appropriate skills, money or a budget, equipment, space, time and so on. On the positive side you are likely to have the commitment of some well meaning volunteers. This might need some channelling but, particularly in voluntary work, this is your biggest asset. On the negative side any or all of time, space and money can be in short supply.

Commonly, we all tend to start out on projects with an optimistic view of the time it will take or a poor estimate of the special skills needed or the financing. Using a grid, such as the one illustrated in Figure 4.1, will help you to estimate what you need.

Figure 4.1   Needs and resources grid

Project Title:

Key stages and dates/times	Key skills and people available?	Space, rooms, equipment available?	Costs involved Is money available?
1			
2			
3			
4			

You can see from the grid that projects have to be planned to ensure that all the resources are available at the time you need them. Where resources are tight, one concept that managers can find difficult to grasp is 'satisficing' – that is, doing a job as well as it needs to be done, no more or no less. Not every aspect of a manager's job requires a perfect result, but maybe you'll find a volunteer who thinks the task should be done a little better. Encourage that person!

Planning

Planning is what we all do – or think we do. Planning focuses on *how* we achieve objectives and on how we can best use resources to that end. The starting point is the objective and defining the path towards it requires us to identify at least:

- what tasks need to be carried out
- in what order
- by when
- with what resources.

There are clearly different levels of planning – corporate, operational, project and so on. This section concentrates on, and provides a few useful tools for, the level you are most likely to be working at with volunteers.

Planning processes

If you are planning for a small project the following few steps may be all that are necessary.

1   List the key tasks needed.
2   Set a target date to finish.
3   Decide the order in which tasks should be carried out.
4   Decide whether any tasks or responsibilities can be delegated to volunteers.
5   Select a method of measuring and controlling progress.
6   Schedule tasks to completion on to a project planner.

Using some form of project plan brings several benefits both to yourself and to volunteers. One of the most important benefits is the ability to communicate clearly to others what you expect to happen and the part to be played by others. It is also a useful exercise in clarifying your own thinking – if you can't put the plan in writing for someone else, you might not have thought it through for yourself. It might also have some motivational benefits in that you can monitor your progress – 'tick off' achievements as you go. Finally, a project plan acts as a control mechanism, informing you, for example, when you need to take corrective action or revise your deadline.

Planning tools

One of the simpler tools to use to set down a plan is the *key events approach* which, essentially, is a sequenced and dated list of the important events or actions which should happen. The format of a key event plan should be kept fairly simple but may involve you or others with more detailed activity in order to fulfil the plan.

Figure 4.2 shows a key event plan for a publicity campaign involving the production and distribution of leaflets. Even from this simple example you can see that some activities depend on others. For example, unless the print copy is right you won't accept the leaflets, and if you haven't got the leaflets you won't have the meeting with volunteers to organise their distribution. In some circumstances this delay might be critical – say, if it were linked to your organisation's annual fundraising event. With more complex projects we might use a Gantt chart (see Figure 4.3) to schedule what are called 'critical paths'. This type of chart shows not only what has to happen when but what is contingent upon another action having started or been completed.

Figure 4.2   Key event plan

Helping Hands Charity Key Event Plan Leaflet Campaign	
Date	*Key Event*
1.8.94	Hold design meeting.
5.8.94	Send designs to printer.
10.8.94	Collect designs from printer, check copy.
12.8.94	Volunteer meeting to manage distribution of leaflets, some by post, some hand-delivered.
15.8.94	All leaflets delivered.

Figure 4.3   Gantt chart: Helping Hands Charity leaflet campaign

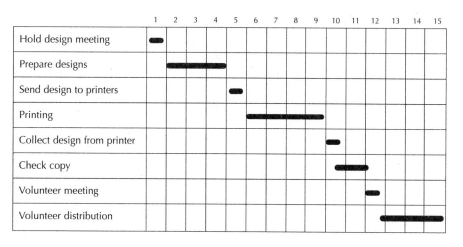

Fundraising – planning in practice

Fundraising is a purposeful activity that needs planning. Indeed, it is the sole purpose of some voluntary organisations. Charity Projects, the organisation behind Comic Relief, is a very successful example and it would be the first to agree that volunteering needs to be properly organised to ensure that its full charitable potential is realised.

Managing the volunteer aspects of fundraising is particularly important. It has been estimated that two-thirds of volunteers are engaged in the fundraising element of voluntary work. However, as there are many other publications devoted entirely to the subject, we will not cover fundraising techniques in detail here and will focus instead on general principles that will help managers working with volunteers in a fundraising setting.

A helpful initial step is for managers and volunteers to look at their activities through a potential donor's eyes. The following exercise is designed to help you develop a perspective of how volunteers may help here.

Exercise 4.4   What makes you give?

- You see someone in the street rattling a tin. What factor makes you decide whether or not you give a donation?
- You receive an envelope through your door. What makes you decide whether or not you will give a donation?

If an appeal envelope comes through your door do you put money in it before the collector returns? If so, is it because you feel obliged to put a few pence in it or do you make rational decisions about which charities you want to support and which ones you don't want to? In both the settings described in the exercise you are more likely to give when asked directly than when not asked. Studies have shown that many people don't give because they haven't been asked. Volunteers need to make the request – they should be shown how to actively ask individuals for donations.

Studies also show that giving is a fairly irrational process. Successful campaigns appeal to people's emotions rather than their analytical abilities. Many people would put money into any tin rattled under their nose at the mention of cats, horses or children – possibly in that order! Here the guidelines for volunteers are straightforward: keep the message simple, make it visual and appealing if possible, and focus on the benefits you deliver – for example, 'Help restore children's sight in India' or 'Save lives at sea'.

Finally, research shows that when people give, they consider that they are making an investment. Their two principal concerns are whether the money will reach its destination and how much of it will actually be spent where it will do some good. The implications of this for volunteers are first that their manner and appearance, backed up by identification if necessary, should inspire trust and also that they should be able to explain how the money is being spent.

Many organisations depend directly on volunteers for their fundraising efforts. This can have both advantages and disadvantages. You may be fortunate to have many volunteers to call on but coordinating their efforts may need a full-scale planning operation. On the other hand, some people may feel more disposed to give to volunteers because they may be convinced by their commitment.

To prepare volunteers for a fundraising activity you need to coach them in:

- approaching people in a professional way
- clearly asking for donations
- showing a little persistence
- explaining how the money is spent
- explaining how efficiently the money is spent
- saying thank you.

These may all seem obvious, but we are considering the activity from the donor's perspective. First they want to be sure the money they give will end up where it is supposed to; second, they appreciate a friendly manner, reasonable appearance, a smile and thanks. Donors are likely to remember not being thanked for their generosity long after they have forgotten which cause they gave to.

Finally, don't forget to use volunteers as a resource in themselves. Collectively they may have far more ideas about fundraising methods than you have and, if given the initiative, will be more enthusiastic to implement those ideas.

Key personal skills

Managing stress

Stress is a significant part of our everyday lives. For some it is a status symbol; it signifies that they have achieved something, that they are busy, committed and involved. Although the term is commonly used, it does not have the same meaning for everyone. Most of us have read articles on the subject and have probably completed stress checklists in the popular press. But while a level of stress stimulates us to achieve success and our personal goals, prolonged exposure can be dysfunctional to our job and relationships and harmful to our health.

Here, we offer you some ways of identifying the effects of personal stress and stress in your organisation and of coping with stress not only to benefit yourself but also your colleagues.

Personal stress

How do you know when you are suffering from stress? Try the following exercise.

Exercise 4.5   How does stress affect me?

Spend a few minutes making a list of how you think stress affects you.
   You have probably included some of the following in your list:

Headaches	Irritability
Frequent tiredness	Poor concentration
Feeling tense	Work avoidance
Sweating	Increased smoking
Feeling anxious	Increased use of alcohol
Stomach disorders	Disturbed sleep

It is important to realise that the items you wrote down above are symptoms – the signs you hopefully recognise before you have the nervous breakdown you've been working towards! They are not causes. Stress is really the state of tension resulting from a range of physical and psychological body responses to stressors or threatening stimuli. These reactions are the body's normal 'fight or flight' response to threats, which shuts down unnecessary bodily activity in order to concentrate all of its energy on activity essential to survival. These reactions are designed as a short-term response to danger; because our bodies are not designed to be in a permanent state of tension, prolonged reactions to a stressor(s) will have a detrimental effect on our lives.

Stress in the organisation

Work itself, whether paid or unpaid, can contribute to a person's stress level. Some occupations are recognised as having a greater stress level than others. One survey of occupational stress ratings indicates the following on a scale of 1–10:

Finance	Accountancy	4.3	Banking	3.7	Stockbroker	5.5
Management	Management	5.8	Personnel	6.0	Secretary	4.7

Communications	Journalism	7.5	Librarian	2.0	Photographer	4.6
Health	Nurse	6.5	Doctor	6.8	Pharmacist	4.5
Environmental	Farmer	4.8	Forestry	4.8	Horticulture	3.8
Uniformed	Police	7.7	Firefighter	6.3	Ambulance	6.3
Caring	Teacher	6.2	Church	3.5	Social work	6.0

Although we have found no examples of work on stress in the voluntary sector there is no reason for managers and volunteers to be exempt. People who work in close teams or groups transfer their own stress to others. The closeness of a group may of itself produce stressful situations for the whole group, called 'group stress'. At work have you noticed increased tension, negativism, arguments or the blaming of others, particularly absent colleagues? Under stress people may adopt difficult and sometimes immature behaviour – clock-watching, creating extra rules, working in isolation, destructive behaviour, cancelling appointments and so on – which leads to further friction in the group.

Constant exposure to stressors can result in a condition known as 'burn-out'. One author described individuals suffering from burn-out thus:

> Their lives seemed to lose meaning, they were often unable to get on with family and friends, were disillusioned with their marriages and careers, tired, frustrated and forced to give increasing amounts of energy to maintain the pace they had set themselves. (Freudenberger and Richardson, 1980:28)

Coping with stress

There are ways in which you, as a manager, can work towards managing stress and so help yourself and those whom you manage. First you should recognise that the workplace has certain inherent stressors. Below are two lists: common workplace stress promoters and stress reducers. Work at reducing these promoters and implementing the stress reducers for both yourself and your volunteers.

1 Common stress promoters

- staff shortages and staff absences which place extra demands on others
- individual excessive workload
- poor communication and poor relationships with other workers
- frequent organisational change
- poor or indifferent management styles
- inadequate training or preparation for the role
- unpleasant working environment
- intrinsic hazards of the job
- conflicts of home, family and work
- poor time management.

2   **Stress reducers**

- effective and sympathetic management
- good communication and relationships
- clarity of job purpose
- training and support for role
- regular feedback on performance
- accessible support network
- having adequate time for the job.

In the next exercise we try to make the identification of workplace stressors more personal to you.

Exercise 4.6   Personal workplace stressors

Identify as many stressors as you can in your workplace under each heading given below.

1   **Job-specific stressors**
(e.g. intense physical activity, emotional strain, being completely desk-bound, being a manager of volunteers!)
2   **Role ambiguity**
(e.g. being unsure of your role or what you are supposed to achieve)
3   **Role conflict**
(e.g. trying to balance efficiency with compassion, or management with hands-on work)
4   **Work load**
(e.g. too much, too little, major fluctuations)
5   **Interpersonal relationships**
(e.g. arguments, poor meetings)
6   **The environment**
(e.g. the culture and the physical environment, parking, decor etc.)

When you've identified your stressors consider whether they have any significant stressful effect on you or your work. Write these effects down too. Do you think the stressors are affecting anyone else at work? Other managers? Volunteers? Recognising that you are subjected to stress is in itself part of addressing the problems and achieving solutions. One odd thing about stress is that we recognise it much more easily in others than in ourselves.

In dealing with the issues you identified above a useful first step is to try to choose different actions for each of them. We have designed the next exercise to help with this.

Exercise 4.7   Stress action plan

Try placing each of the stressors that you have previously listed into one of the following three categories:

1   **Immediate action:** Issues which you can begin to tackle immediately or within a very short time frame.
2   **Future action:** Issues which are not too urgent and which you consider can be solved either by yourself or in consultation with others also affected by the stressor(s). You must accept that it may take time to see a result.
3   **Adaptation:** Issues which you will have to tackle using a completely different approach – for example, negotiating a change in your responsibilities, changing your office hours.

In choosing something to do first, go for something you'll succeed at. Failing will only add to your stress. Think about adaptation – it is the hardest skill for a manager to achieve since we tend to think about solving things in a direct way not laterally. But adaptation is a significant human trait, otherwise we wouldn't be here. When we successfully adapt to change we often experience a positive boost. Ignoring a stressor isn't usually helpful, but may be legitimate if it is something you feel unable to influence.

Finally we will list some of the more general things you can do, or advise volunteers to do, to help manage stress:

- Make sure you get sufficient sleep for your needs.
- Eat a healthy, well balanced diet.
- Take adequate exercise, at least the equivalent of a two-mile walk twice a week, or take up swimming.
- Practise relaxation exercises.
- Dissipate anger as quickly as possible by vigorous exercise.
- Express your emotions.
- Learn to be assertive (not aggressive).
- Try to see the issue or problem from the other person's perspective.
- Learn to compromise.
- Avoid overdependence on alcohol or tobacco.
- Take control of your time – keep a time log.
- Try to help others.
- Seek counselling support before things get worse.

Managing time

You may be trying to balance home and family commitments with the demands of a managerial role in the voluntary sector and support a number of staff and volunteers. The objective of all dedicated working managers should be to analyse thoroughly all situations, anticipate all problems prior to their occurrence, have answers for these problems and move swiftly to solve these problems whenever called upon. *All pigs fed and ready to fly!*

When we looked at stress we identified poor management of time and of other people's demands on us as significant stressors. Think back to a recent working day. What did you actually achieve? We often feel tired at the end of the day; we know we've worked hard. But did we achieve what we set out to in the time we allowed? When we consider more deeply we will recall the numerous telephone interruptions, the visitors to the office or the clients who called in to make enquiries. We may also remember not having much of a plan, the search for the lost file or letter, or the meeting that started late and overran.

Good time management is about how we organise our work and how we prioritise it. Yet, the sheer daunting load can prevent us from even considering prioritising it. We end up lurching from one crisis to another and skimping on the important jobs we should do. This pattern, in turn, creates more stress and may lead to burn-out. Any approach to improving time management must recognise the wider stressors.

Exercise 4.8   What do we spend time worrying about?

As we discussed earlier, stress is a significant factor in our lives, and certain stressors may be identified with the workplace. Look back at the responses you gave in Exercise 4.7. Make an estimate below of how much time per week you spend worrying about them.

1   job-specific stressors
2   role ambiguity
3   role conflict
4   workload
5   interpersonal relationships
6   the environment.

What takes up the most time? Is the amount of time in any way proportionate to the amount of grief it causes you? When we address time management we must take these stressors into account. We are fairly sure that you will have ascribed some of your management constraints to some of these headings.

Now let us look at a few practical ways which might help you manage your time more effectively. A helpful system to prioritise work is to rate jobs as A, B or C.

- **A:** jobs rated A are critical jobs. If you fail to meet their deadlines you will encounter substantial problems. Drop everything for these.
- **B:** jobs rated B are urgent. They need doing but the consequences are not too severe if you breach a deadline. Work on these as soon as time becomes available.
- **C:** jobs rated C are neither urgent nor critical. They can be tackled when you can find the time.

After prioritising all your work, consider whether you can delegate elements of the job to others. Delegation is a key aspect of effective time management, yet it is a skill which managers frequently find difficult to apply. We tackle this in the checklist below.

Checklist: Time management tips

Better daily organisation of your workload may also be achieved by using some of the following time management tips.

1 Reserve the first and last hour of the day for yourself to tackle key issues without interruption. During this time, delegate your telephone calls and routine work.
2 Encourage an appointment system. This is fair to both yourself and those who wish to see you.
3 Ensure that all meetings have an agenda and that the start and finish times are known to those attending. Do not wait for late arrivals nor reiterate earlier business for people arriving late. They can read the minutes afterwards, and it may encourage them to be more punctual next time.
4 Review your office routine and systems. Much time is wasted searching for misplaced important documents. Make sure that you have an easily accessed filing system and bring forward system.
5 Start your day by listing what you intend to achieve. Label them A, B or C using the system above. Check whether there are any activities that you could delegate. Try not to do any C activities before finishing the A activities.
6 Come in early rather than stay late.
7 Keep your door open if you don't mind interruptions, but close it to signify you don't want them.

Delegating to others

Managers often experience problems with delegation – they think they can do the job better themselves, they can't trust anyone else, it's the fun part of the job, they dare not ask, they'll be seen as unpopular for dumping work on others and so on. However, delegating is rather more complex than offloading all the unpopular bits of the job that we don't want to do ourselves. There is a balance between responsibility and autonomy to consider. Ultimately we remain responsible for all the tasks we delegate, which will obviously influence what we are prepared to delegate and to whom. *Delegation is not abdication.*

But if we wish to delegate successfully we have to delegate some autonomy with the task to enable the other person to make decisions about how to do it best. Good delegating serves two purposes. We, as managers, benefit from having tasks done and gaining the time to spend on other matters. Those to whom we delegate should find the allotted task rewarding, with some degree of motivating challenge. This is better achieved by delegating tasks which carry the responsibility for setting objectives, planning the work and getting the job done. The delegated task should come complete with the power to make necessary decisions.

Very much related to the balance above is control and trust. We feel we have more control over those aspects of the job we don't delegate and may worry about how well the delegated aspects are being done. If we cannot develop trust in others our efforts to delegate are unlikely to be successful. We will waste time by continually checking up on progress. Here we need to exercise our judgement in picking the right person for the right job. Trust is also fragile – once broken it cannot be rebuilt to the same extent. A danger is that we use delegation as a way of controlling what people do, rather than getting tasks done. We tend also to develop trust in longer-term working relationships.

Do you believe there are any particular difficulties or constraints in delegating to volunteers? Their available time may be an issue but should be overcome by asking first if they have the time to undertake a particular task as part of the commitment. Lack of knowledge, skills or training may also limit your choice. This is not strictly a volunteer limitation but a lack of investment.

Set out below are some helpful guidelines for better delegation.

Checklist: Ten steps to better delegation

1   Define what needs to be done and give responsibility for doing it.
2   Explain why it needs to be done and why it's important to you.

3   Explain what standard you expect.
4   Agree a deadline.
5   Ensure the person has all the resources they need and access to anything they haven't got.
6   Inform relevant others that you have delegated the task.
7   State if/when you will be monitoring or expect to see progress to date.
8   Wait for results. Don't step in too soon.
9   Ensure you have an adequate control system.
10 Thank everyone involved, praise successful achievement and help people learn from their mistakes.

Assertiveness

Another important self-management skill is assertiveness. This is a skill that we need to learn and practice if we are to avoid unnecessary tension and stress in working with others. Assertion should not be confused with aggression which is a negative response to a situation, usually guaranteed to stimulate a like response.

Assertiveness involves:

- standing up for your own rights in such a way that you do not violate another person's rights
- expressing your needs, wants, opinions, feelings and beliefs in direct, honest and appropriate ways.

In being assertive, we must acknowledge that everyone has a basic right to assert themselves. Anne Dickinson (1982) lists the following rights which are shared by everyone:

I have the right to state my own needs and set my own priorities as a person, independent of any roles that I may assume in my life
I have the right to be treated with respect as an intelligent, capable and equal human being.
I have a right to express my feelings.
I have a right to express my opinions and values.
I have a right to say yes or no for myself.
I have a right to make mistakes.
I have a right to change my mind.
I have a right to say I do not understand.
I have a right to ask for what I want.
I have a right to decline responsibility for other people's problems.
I have a right to deal with others without being dependent on them for approval.

Exercise 4.9   How do assertive people behave?

If you were to observe someone being assertive how do you think they would behave?

An assertive person would probably:

- look other people in the eye
- use an 'adult' tone of voice when making requests
- avoid adopting 'childish' defence mechanisms
- accept that they will not always agree with others
- express views positively but not dogmatically
- express emotion appropriately in making choices.

Some of the factors which help us to develop assertiveness are:

- being self-confident and having a positive frame of mind
- an appreciation of other people's points of view
- a work environment that encourages discussion
- an ability to take risks
- clarity of views and values.

Factors which prevent us being assertive include:

- lack of clarity about personal views and values
- lack of opportunity to be assertive
- other people's aggression
- the structure of the organisation
- the role which you are playing.

The best way to develop assertiveness skills is to practise them. If you are reluctant to try out these skills within your organisation, then consider enrolling on a course. These are often offered in local colleges and usually involve developing skills and confidence in role-play situations which are safe ways to learn, and will benefit many areas of your life.

You can begin to be assertive today. Take control of your own time, review how you currently manage it and seek new ways in which to make better use of this scarce commodity.

5 Managing volunteers as individuals

The special needs of volunteers

Volunteers have special needs of which managers, particularly those in paid employment, should be more aware. While generalising about these needs may not give due recognition to every volunteer's unique situation, we can offer you some useful guidelines. Volunteers are your most important resource and they need particular kinds of support; recognising their needs is essential to get the best out of working together.

First and foremost is the recognition that volunteers have important other relationships and activities in their lives – partners, family, employers and friends, hobbies, commitments and so on. These all compete for a volunteer's time and therefore the contribution they can make. In turn, the demands you make on them can affect their relationships with others. Human relationships are complex and a pleasant or unpleasant experience may be easily transferred, sometimes unknowingly, into other relationships.

The starting point for recognising that volunteers have particular needs is at their initial interview. As a good manager you will have discussed with them the realistic time commitment they can make. Make sure that you are not asking too much of a busy person. Ask how their family or their partner views this commitment. You may feel like responding that volunteers are adults and, as such, can make their own decisions, but our experience shows that some do not always give due consideration to the consequences for their relationships. Natural enthusiasm will lead you to encourage as many volunteers as possible to 'sign on the dotted line', but you need to be cautious lest you take an overoptimistic volunteer who may let you down. Conversely, beware of volunteers becoming so involved with their voluntary interest that their partners feel neglected. Keep your knowledge of volunteers' circumstances up-to-date in a non-intrusive way by simply maintaining regular contact, asking how they are doing and being receptive to their reply.

As a manager of volunteers you accept some responsibility for them, and for the effect your organisation has on them. Be aware of the time that people are giving to the organisation and, where appropriate, be prepared to discuss informally with them whether or not they might be overdoing it. This may cause you some apprehension, but perhaps not so much as suddenly losing a valuable volunteer because of pressure of work. One way of recognising the contribution of partners and family is by involving them in the social aspects of your organisation and making them feel a part of it, without obligation. This may be achieved by regular social events as well as having an open door for the family.

Another particular need is for good quality training, appropriate to the role they will fulfil. Again, you should take into account the value of the volunteer's time which is precious and should not be wasted. Also, if volunteers spend time on inappropriate training it removes them from the service that they originally joined your organisation to provide. Training itself falls into two groups, in-house or external to your organisation. In-house training may involve formal events such as arranged lectures, workshops and so on, or on-the-job approaches such as attachments to key people. We describe one approach in more detail, giving experience, later in this chapter. For most volunteers the larger part of their initial training needs can probably be managed in-house, although this should not serve as an excuse for poor quality training. Some check needs to be made with volunteers regarding the methods and relevance of the training given.

Inappropriate training often happens because induction requires volunteers to listen to someone 're-inventing the wheel'. Volunteers have often attained certain skills in their usual employment, either by qualification or experience, and are then required to sit through the same process in order to carry out their voluntary work. This evident disrespect for individuals can be overcome in a number of ways, by informal assessment of individual's needs, by identifying gaps for which they can be given selective training, by use of selected distance-learning materials, and by partnering new volunteers with experienced ones. Treating everyone as universally uninformed may so disillusion people that they do not wish to stay with the organisation.

Finally, the National Vocational Qualification (NVQ) scheme is now utilised within many care schemes and organisations. It is a scheme which recognises the learning experience that people may have gained from their everyday work. There is no reason why volunteers should not benefit from obtaining a qualification based upon their work within your organisation. Such a qualification will not only give your organisation a quality perspective, but may enable people who are unemployed to give and gain experience as volunteers which in turn may lead to employment. Details of such schemes will usually be available from local colleges or area Training and

Enterprise Councils (TECs) and, where accompanied by formal recognition of prior experience, can serve as a useful extra recruiting attraction.

Who volunteers?

Various research projects have examined both the type of person who gives voluntary service and people's reasons for volunteering. Volunteers are engaged in a very diverse range of voluntary work – trustees, fundraisers, governors, helpers, non-executives, gardeners. The 35–44 year-old age group is most likely to volunteer and will spend an average of about three hours per week on voluntary work. There is a close link with social position: some 75 per cent of those in managerial and professional positions say they do voluntary work, 58 per cent in skilled manual work and 37 per cent in unskilled occupations. Surprisingly, the data shows that retired people are the least likely to volunteer.

Some of the more common reasons for volunteering are:

- having free time
- wishing to help others
- a wish for social contact
- identification of an explicit need of help
- a wish to gain experience prior to salaried work
- religious and spiritual reasons
- unemployment and a wish to fill time positively
- political motives – for example, a desire to tackle a particular social problem
- a wish for friendship.

This list is not exhaustive, but serves to identify the wide range of motivations expressed by volunteers when offering their time. Martin Knapp suggests that volunteers may be trying to

> ... fit some normative expectation of behaviour, to gain prestige or social approval for participation, or to expand their social circle. There may be therapeutic or rehabilitative reasons for volunteering: to help cope with inner anxieties and uncertainties about personal worth: to feel needed. (Knapp, 1990:8)

Clearly managers should develop an understanding of what motivates each individual through regular contact and attempt to use that insight when considering what roles each volunteer could undertake.

We will leave you with the following notice which was left on the noticeboard of a national voluntary organisation by a volunteer following attendance at a course. Use it to check against what you do in your organisation.

The seven deadly sins of directing volunteers

1   To recruit a volunteer for a course or programme in which you do not believe or to ask a volunteer to do a job you wouldn't do yourself.
2   To worry about the number of volunteers you need to the degree that you sign a person up even if he or she is not right for the job to be done.
3   To restrict a volunteer's effectiveness by not providing adequate preparation, training or tools.
4   To ask salaried staff to work as a team with volunteers if you yourself do not have volunteers helping with the responsibilities of your job.
5   To be so concerned about your own job security that you do not stand up and fight for the needs and rights of the volunteers you represent.
6   To offer volunteers certain opportunities and working conditions and then not deliver.
7   To waste a volunteer's time – EVER.

Improving communication

In Chapter 1 we drew attention to the importance of good communication as an essential first principle to good management. We have all experienced the effects of poor communications in one way or another. You can probably think of a recent example where a shortfall in your performance was due to poor communication. For any organisation to be successful it must communicate clearly, both internally and outwardly. This must be both the responsibility of every manager and built in to the mechanics of the organisation.

Everyone agrees about this in theory, but in practice it doesn't always happen. You are probably very familiar with the difficulties faced when trying to communicate within your organisation to volunteers: many volunteers are not available weekdays between 9a.m. and 5p.m.; some do not have a telephone; you can't ring them at work; you're not at work when they ring in; the organisation may meet in full only once a month and volunteers may have difficulty attending those meetings that do exist due to work and family commitments.

The following exercise will help you to assess communications in your organisation.

Exercise 5.1   Communications audit

Think about the following communications questions in your organisation.

1   What opportunities exist for volunteers to communicate with each other?
2   Are meetings seen primarily as social events or as business meetings?
3   How well is the meeting agenda put together and managed at the meeting?
4   What proportion of your team attends regularly?
5   Are there regular attenders and some who attend infrequently?
6   Are key messages summarised at meetings verbally or in writing?
7   What other methods apart from meetings do you use to communicate with volunteers?

The most common responses we hear to the above questions are that meetings are the most common form of communication. Attendance at meetings fluctuates, but there is rarely a full turn-out. Managers may have difficulties both in managing meetings and finding other ways to communicate with those who don't regularly attend. Below we give some suggestions on:

- managing meetings
- using display boards
- using newsletters
- developing personal contact.

Managing meetings

Meetings should have a social element as this encourages teamwork and may be the rare occasion when some volunteers see each other. But they do need to be structured around a planned agenda. Plan early so that volunteers can contribute to the agenda and it can be distributed before the meeting confirming the venue and time. Aim for most of the business to be on the agenda and not categorised as 'any other business'.

Meetings usually have one of three aims: *to generate ideas, give information or make decisions*. When you are actually running the meeting you should encourage everyone to contribute actively to whichever of these issues is being discussed. Hear everybody's ideas and make sure everyone has understood the information given out. Effective communication is a two-way and dynamic process. Even when you think you are just giving information do not deprive yourself of feedback from others.

Making decisions should be done more slowly, possibly spread over more than one meeting. Try to ensure that everyone participates in making decisions so that some ownership is achieved. Decisions should be minuted, those agreeing to implement them should be identified against agreed dates, and the minutes should be circulated as soon as possible after the meeting.

Some other general points will add to the success of your meetings. Try to make infrequent attenders feel equally welcome – spend time with them not just your close associates. Try to follow the agenda and keep the meeting to time. Try to give important items sufficient time – don't sweep them aside or say you'll come back to them if you don't intend to. Try to listen in to the informal discussion over refreshments either during or after the meeting; use this opportunity to pick up on issues that people aren't happy to mention formally. You need to make sure you have given volunteers time to express their concerns and that you have some way of getting your key message to them.

There may be ways you can improve attendance by thinking about the venue, the time and the size of the meeting.

1   **The venue**

- How accessible is the venue, particularly to those without their own transport?
- Is it a safe venue particularly for those who travel alone?
- Is it welcoming and comfortable?

2   **The time of the meeting**

- Do you know what time is preferable for most attenders?
- If late, does it finish at a reasonable hour for people to travel home safely?

3   **The size of the meeting**

- How many people come? The larger it is the better managed it has to be. If there are 40 or 50 it is difficult to do more than give information. Making effective decisions may be better done with smaller meetings.

These points may appear very basic, but some are often overlooked even by the most experienced managers. They do take that little bit of extra effort in our busy schedules.

Display boards

Although printed material has its limitations compared with a conversation, used thoughtfully it can assist with good communication and provides a record to refer to. Ensure that you have a well-presented display board for circulars and posters in a visible area at your branch. It should be at a busy place, a main corridor or the staff meeting room, for example. Consider its appeal, its size and height, the presentation of material displayed, the use of colour and different layouts. Try to find someone who will take responsibility for keeping it up-to-date and taking old notices down. The latter is something you might easily delegate to someone who has time and commitment to make it a success.

Newsletters

Similarly, newsletters should be visually attractive and stimulating to read. A small group of dedicated people sharing the work of collating information, printing and distributing the end product can often produce a very effective result. A good product quarterly is better than a poor product monthly. Ensure that you keep to schedule and that people anticipate its arrival. Encourage participation with articles, no matter how small, and consider a reader's page. Think about how to distribute newsletters widely; it may be worthwhile sending them to volunteers' home addresses. Nothing beats personal communication, however, so don't rely entirely on print.

Personal contact

Those who can't attend regular meetings may lose out both on information essential to working effectively and the social dimension. A good strategy is to meet with these volunteers, listen to them and give information on matters likely to affect the organisation and their position within it. By such contact you can convey that you value them and possibly discover reasons for their difficulty in coming to meetings.

Volunteers like to feel valued and part of a team providing a much needed service. As managers of volunteers we must endeavour to provide the volunteer with a quality support network which goes beyond information-giving and encompasses their personal needs.

Giving support

If you have been a volunteer yourself you will appreciate that there have been times when you have needed support. It may have been from your manager, other volunteers, your family or friends, or others detached from the organisation. You may have also needed different kinds of support from different people – general encouragement, praise, advice, someone to listen to you, someone to share a problem with, or perhaps someone with special skills to resolve a specific issue. But did you always get it when you needed it? In our experience, managers of volunteers sadly do not always recognise that volunteers need support and that they need to help.

Many employers recognise their responsibilities in providing support to their workers with work-related difficulties. They tend to recognise the more obvious situations like the stress of working with victims of traumatic incidents but are poor at recognising the effects of prolonged contact with distressing or demanding situations. Examples of the latter may be:

- working with homeless people living rough on the streets
- working with newly arrived refugees who are separated from their families or victims of malnutrition or torture
- visiting aged and sick people in their homes who have little money and receive minimal statutory care services.

In this work climate volunteers may become tired, frustrated, disillusioned, angry, resentful and feel inadequate and powerless. If left unsupported they may leave the organisation, often without you knowing why, or they may continue but at personal risk to their own health. The build-up to a volunteer resigning or becoming less effective through work pressure is often insidious. Without structured support it may well go unnoticed both by colleagues and managers.

Exercise 5.2   Giving support

Consider the following scenario.

Peter is a fairly new volunteer involved in emergency aid. He is on duty at a local motor cycling event when a motorbike leaves the road at high speed . The rider is severely injured and later dies with a broken neck. Three of the crowd are also injured and need first aid.

Peter, on completion of his duties for that day, returns home to his family. Peter has difficulty talking about what happened to his wife. He keeps thinking back on the situation, visualising the scene, analysing what he did and wondering whether he could have acted quicker or more effectively. Did the rider have to die with neck injuries? Was it because of how Peter handled him?

The outcome may be displayed in his behaviour or actions to those around him. He may be critical of his skills or those of others. He may be critical of the training he had or the partner he worked with. Others may not appreciate the underlying cause and may not therefore be in a position to respond in a supportive manner.

How should we improve our support of Peter or others in similar situations?

We can start by ensuring that we give volunteers training that makes them competent and confident to do what we ask of them. Initial training should explain to volunteers how and where support is available – from their manager, from a mentor or supervisor, or by peer group support.

As managers of volunteers we should ensure volunteers receive ongoing support. We need to provide good briefing and debriefing for volunteers when they are involved in potentially demanding situations. We also examined some of the ways managers can support themselves in Chapter 4. These principles can be transferred to supporting others, as can some of the skills we shall examine in Chapters 6 and 7.

We believe strongly that it is important to build support mechanisms into the way you operate from the outset. This avoids the possibility at a later date of your attempts at support being misinterpreted as interference at best or criticism at worst. Giving support to the individual must be seen as part of everyone's responsibility, not just the manager's. This prepares an individual volunteer to acknowledge his or her own needs, to be alert for signs of need in others, and to offer time to support colleagues.

If you have managerial responsibilities for volunteers consider learning some basic helping and facilitation skills to improve your support skills. If such training is undertaken in a work group it will assist in team-building. In itself this will enable people to feel safe and share matters of anxiety and concern. Smaller organisations may not have the in-house resources to offer back-up when required. Here managers need to develop networks with other local organisations or develop links with external, independent, professional services.

There are further approaches you can take at a local level. Involving friends and family of volunteers in the organisation in an informal, social way will help them understand some of the pressures that volunteers encounter. There should be no pressure to join. In this way you may avoid the possibility of resentment where a loved one appears to spend all of their free time with your group. They will identify colleagues and will be more likely to recognise you should you need later to work with them in supporting a family member.

There may be times when a volunteer does not attend for a long period of time, perhaps due to illness, work or family pressures, or possibly disillusionment with their role as a volunteer. Many volunteer managers feel uneasy making home visits, fearing that this may be seen as intrusive. Perhaps we could look at it from the volunteer's, or their family's, viewpoint. Your failure to make contact could well be interpreted as being uncaring or ungrateful for the services the member has given. Even in the most caring of organisations, it can be very difficult for an individual to gain the confidence to return after a lengthy break. Your contact could well prevent the loss of a valuable volunteer.

Similarly where a person is experiencing difficulties in balancing their voluntary commitment and home–work commitments it may be useful to suggest a period of absence from 'front-line' voluntary work. However, make sure you retain contact throughout the period and that he or she is encouraged to attend social and any business activities which they feel able to cope with.

Your support, as a manager, will be equally as important in respect of volunteers who seem to be overcommitted. You should keep a weather eye on those who give a greater than normal amount of their time to voluntary work. It may be wise to consider any underlying reason for their degree of commitment. Once again, it may not be easy to broach the subject but, as a manager, you have a duty to your organisation and the individual concerned to ensure that, in the long term, no ill-effect is caused to either party. Support of the individual is enshrined in your overall managerial role and should be ever-present in managing the delivery of service. Your volunteers are your most valuable resource – expensive in terms of training and the experience which they amass and extremely difficult to replace.

Motivating others

To manage other people effectively we need to understand what motivates their activities, and therefore how we can influence that motivation. There are probably more theories about motivation in management literature than any other aspect of management. We will briefly discuss the ideas of three psychologists.

Abraham Maslow

The motivation theory most people can readily recall is Maslow's hierarchy of needs. Put simply, this states that our behaviour is motivated to fill needs in our lives and that we put needs in a particular order. First we are motivated to satisfy our essential *physical needs*, food, warmth, shelter, comfort and so on. There are four more steps in the hierarchy, *safety and security, sense of belonging, self-esteem* and finally *mental and personal growth*, sometimes called self-actualisation. The theory suggests that people need to be sure their basic needs are going to be met before they can attend to higher-order needs. For example, it would be difficult to invest time learning a new skill when you're worried about being evicted.

As managers we need to consider how volunteers will have their needs satisfied by both membership of a voluntary organisation and involvement in that type of work. We also need to think about how we can help volunteers to satisfy those needs.

Exercise 5.3   Meeting volunteers' needs

Think about the following examples.

You have asked some volunteers to spend the day at a major shopping centre collecting funds in tins and giving out flags/stickers. Are you sure they will be able to get lunch, shelter if it rains, have access to a public toilet? Could you arrange a packed lunch for them? Yes, these are simple physical needs but, if they're not met, then not much work will be done!

At one of your team meetings a volunteer says she can't attend the evening meetings any more because her husband doesn't think it is safe. One or two other members of the meeting start jeering at her about being under his thumb etc. She is concerned about both her physical safety at night and now her psychological safety in the group. You may need to intervene on her behalf.

You are asked to pick a team from your volunteers to staff a charity stall at a major local event. It will be a real opportunity to raise awareness of what your group does. Naturally you want to pick those you think will do it well, but you do have a volunteer who particularly needs to feel valued. Could this be a way of improving his sense of belonging? Or even increase his self-confidence?

These kinds of considerations about how to motivate people, or at least not demotivate them, are not difficult to consider but we should not overlook them.

Douglas McGregor

Another way of looking at how we might motivate people is based on our assumptions about how people behave at work. Douglas McGregor (1960) had a theory that managers could be divided into two types with opposing views about managing their staff, based on the assumptions they have about them. He termed these 'Theory X' and 'Theory Y' managers.

1   *Theory X assumptions about human behaviour*:

- Most people generally have an inherent dislike of work and try to avoid it.
- Therefore most people need to be controlled, coerced or threatened with punishment to force them to make an effort.
- Most people actually prefer to be directed and don't want responsibility. What they do is guided by seeking security rather than ambition.

2   *Theory Y assumptions about human behaviour*:

- Most ordinary people do not inherently dislike work; it can be a source of satisfaction.
- Most people will take on self-direction if they have some commitment to the objectives.
- If the conditions are right, people will accept and seek responsibility.
- A great deal more people could offer creative ideas and solutions than normally do so.

Reassuringly, McGregor was an advocate of Theory Y approaches. This is not idle theory, though, as one of these sets of assumptions may predominate in your organisation. Can you identify certain managers who lean towards one type or another? If so, do you think it affects how the volunteers they work with respond to them? The theory should also tell you something about how to motivate volunteers – for example, by removing unnecessary constraints and asking volunteers for their ideas. Another valuable aspect that this theory demonstrates is that people respond to the way they are managed. If you don't show you are looking for responsibility from a volunteer you probably won't get it; conversely, if you tell people you value what they are thinking, they are more likely to share their ideas with you.

Frederick Hertzberg

Another useful theory is from Frederick Hertzberg. He tried to identify factors about jobs which satisfied workers and those which dissatisfied them. The most commonly cited 'satisfiers' were achievement and recognition; the most common 'dissatisfier' was disagreement with company policy and administration. There are some clear messages for managers here in helping volunteers to be 'satisfied' with what they do. First we must structure what we ask volunteers to do to give them a sense of achievement. Second, we need to give them due recognition for their achievements. Lastly, we should enable them to carry out their job without too much bureaucratic interference.

Hertzberg's ideas stimulate managers to focus on what they can actually do to enrich volunteers' jobs. There should be more to volunteering in your organisation than making tea and stuffing envelopes. Do you think that volunteers experience their activities in your organisation as meaningful?

Exercise 5.4   A well-designed job?

List what you think are the key components of a well-designed job.
There is considerable agreement that a job should:

- constitute some sort of whole – be an identifiable, complete task
- be seen by the volunteer as worth doing (therefore possibly needing explanation)
- let the volunteer take the decisions necessary to complete the job
- give a measure of feedback by its own completion
- give fair reward for the effort involved.

These general theories of motivation should give us specific help in managing volunteers. Every volunteer will have their own individual reason for why they do what they do, as will, of course, managers. The manager's job is to try to understand the individual motivations of their team and find ways of both satisfying them and meeting his wider objectives. While the reasons for becoming a volunteer hopefully have a degree of altruistic intent – wanting to help others – they may include wanting to meet other people, to develop skills, to relieve boredom, to gain new experiences or to increase a sense of belonging in the local community. We must be receptive to all these needs.

We could ask about how your organisation motivates volunteers, but another useful way of looking at this issue is to ask why volunteers leave your organisation. If the reasons are analysed in any systematic way you may find indications of how your organisation is failing them; this is covered in more detail in Chapter 7.

Improving negotiation skills

Relying on volunteers to do everything out of a sense of deep personal fulfilment, or just because you want it done, will at best yield patchy results. Not every task that needs doing is either easy or popular and, at times, the reason for undertaking it will not even be understood. Consequently, you will sometimes need to use negotiation skills to achieve a particular outcome.

Negotiation is the process of achieving the best possible agreement between you and the other party(ies). You may be trying to resolve an issue between just you and a volunteer, or it may involve other volunteers, another manager or a customer. The basic skills of negotiation may be used in many other settings – resolving a complaint, managing conflict, or improving teamwork, for example. The outcome of a successful negotiation is that all parties agree, are happy and can commit themselves to resolving an issue and the necessary action required. This is often referred to as a 'win–win' situation.

If you negotiate too toughly you might initially feel you have achieved exactly what you want. However, if the other party feels dissatisfied then the agreement may not last very long and you will soon be back at the beginning having wasted a lot of time. You should aim for a more enduring and mutually agreeable outcome from the outset.

You should consider the following in preparing for a negotiation:

- Be sure what you want to achieve from the negotiation.
- Make sure you have a 'start' position – an ideal outcome – and a position beyond which you will not move.
- Know what you will concede and what you will not.
- Try to concede only in exchange for concessions from the other party.
- Try to find out as much as you can about the other party's position.

When you feel you are prepared, arrange an initial meeting. You may want some notes with you to refer to. During the meeting you should concentrate on trying to achieve the following in the following order.

1 Give all parties an opportunity to express their perspective on the problem – for example, why something won't work, why they can't or won't help, what is preventing them from doing something.
2 Attempt to put these issues in to some sort of shared perspective.
3 Allow all parties to say what they want out of any agreement.
4 Allow all parties to offer as many alternative solutions as they can think of.
5 Encourage all parties to indicate where they think there is room to be flexible or modify their own or another's position.
6 Ask all parties to agree to any final agreement that emerges at the meeting and the particular contribution they will personally make. This may need to be recorded or minuted.
7 Ensure that all parties are satisfied with the outcome or progress made to date.
8 Agree a review date to monitor the progress of the agreement.

This series of steps may sound elaborate for the one-to-one discussions that you might have with individual volunteers but the principles will be the same. You will have to reach a mutually acceptable agreement through a sound understanding of each other's position. You will have to achieve this with minimum personal upset and without jeopardising the volunteer's goodwill. In this respect, try to keep the person and the problem separate – for example, rather than express your concerns about why the volunteer is unwilling to help you can discuss why you each have different interpretations of the job. You will also have to reach the agreement without resort to the sanctions which you might employ in a formal employer–employee situation, and possibly without the rewards also. This is why we feel a good understanding of what motivates each individual volunteer is an absolute necessity. Emphasise these motivations in your negotiating position.

Setting objectives and reviewing performance

In Chapter 3 we made an initial assessment of your role in the organisation, of the importance of planning around objectives to meet that role and of the importance of volunteers as perhaps the single most important resource you have in achieving your objectives. This chapter has brought us nearer to managing important aspects of that relationship between you and volunteers. It has looked at their special needs and how you might give them support and motivate them. It has looked at developing your communication and negotiation skills. In the wider commercial world you may be used to appraisal systems or individual performance reviews as ways in which organisational demands and individual needs can be harnessed together. As a manager in the voluntary sector you have a similar task using different resources.

Setting objectives with volunteers has two functions. The first, and obvious, one is for you both to clarify what the volunteer will do as a contribution to the wider effort. The second is to formulate the agreed objectives into an informal support mechanism in themselves, by both you and the volunteer trying to put some boundaries around what he or she does. Reviewing performance is a continuation of these two themes. First, you both want to know how the volunteer is coping with the agreed objectives, to find out, for example, whether there is a need for further training. Second, it gives the opportunity to review the support he or she needs and whether you are giving enough or the right type of support.

One of the main purposes behind setting objectives and reviewing performance is to create a mechanism with which you can impart a sense of achievement to volunteers. They have some choice and control in the structured way in which they will make a contribution to the wider objectives. You have a mechanism in which you can legitimately discuss this and by which you can convey feedback to them about their performance.

Consider this rather sneaky question. Do you know what all the volunteers are doing in your department? Pick out half a dozen names. What are they working on? How well are they doing at it? Are they doing something of real value to the organisation or wasting time? Who is giving them feedback and support?

We've had conversations like this with some voluntary sector managers:

'What does Bill do here?'

'He usually comes in on Tuesday and Thursday mornings.'

'Yes, but what does he do?'

'He works with Jenny when she comes in later.'

'OK. So what do they do?'

'They both work in Room 6 together.'

'Yes...?'

'Oh, they're quite busy in there, though I'm not too sure what they do in detail. They've both been coming in a long time now. About 10.30 he usually comes out and makes us all a cup of coffee. He's sweet, really, and he did wash up the cups last week. On Thursdays he goes half an hour earlier so he can drop the post off at the main office. We all get on well here.'

We hope this isn't too familiar to you. Bill might be a busy chap but what exactly is he doing *for the organisation*? Does anyone know? Does he have a manager who takes an interest? What happens in Room 6 might be really important, but *who's managing it*?

If you accept the case for setting objectives there is a challenge in how you do it. The tendency is to make the process very formal and unnecessarily bureaucratic. In your past experience it may have been linked to a pay and performance review. For volunteers it obviously won't be pay-related, and there is no need for pages of objectives which are sent off to be ratified by head office or 'grandparents'. You should keep the process as simple as possible, with minimal notes or without reference to anything written down.

In essence you are trying to convey to volunteers that you are interested in them, in what they can do to help the organisation, in what help they need and in what they want for themselves. You want to ensure that their activities have some structure, partly for their own benefit, and partly to make sure that both you and they are using their time to the best possible effect. You want both of you to have an opportunity to say what you are gaining from this working arrangement. As writing too much down may create some confidentiality and storage problems, and should think of some informal ways round this. Much of this is to do with consciously saying to yourself: 'I haven't had a chat with Bill for a few months since we agreed the "Scaling the Eiger" project. I wonder how he's getting on? I'll see if I can find him tomorrow. We may need to sit down together or just have a few words.' Easy, isn't it?

Giving experience

You can never be sure whether volunteers are looking for stability or variety in their voluntary work unless, of course, you ask. Although some may seem perfectly happy doing the same thing day in, day out, take care that you are not taking them for granted. Earlier in this chapter we discussed finding out what motivates the volunteers you work with and about job enrichment. Some may have chosen to volunteer deliberately for the experience, to add to their CV or improve their job prospects. Others may be quite settled but would welcome seeing wider aspects of what you do or welcome a little more variety. For these people you need to consider the experience you are providing.

This issue can perhaps be considered as a return on your investment. Some managers might feel they have little time or obligation to worry about what else volunteers could do. But it may be that investing the time in others will bring returns by them helping you out with different ideas or when you need it most. Traditionally, organisations had fixed roles for all their staff but, nowadays many organisations increasingly ensure that staff are flexible or 'multi-skilled' as it is sometimes referred to. In some manufacturing organisations staff may work in teams where everyone can do everyone else's job, for example. Other organisations at least consider short-term job swaps or attachments to other departments. Do you do anything like this in your organisation, even with the paid staff?

We're not suggesting that you need anything elaborate for volunteers to widen their experience. Try thinking about everything in which you are personally involved where it might help you to have a volunteer involved too. This need not necessarily be to do a lot of the work but just to broaden their understanding of what you and the organisation are doing.

Exercise 5.5   Giving volunteers experience

To do this in a more structured way take a look at all the appointments in your diary for the next four weeks. Is there any meeting or visit that it would help a volunteer to attend? Would they get a better insight into the workings of the organisation? Could you apply this to any other manager's activities? Could you arrange for volunteers to team up together for a project or swap jobs for a week or so?

Using some thought it is possible in quite small ways to provide volunteers with a variety of experience which helps them to broaden and deepen their contribution to the organisation. One of the principles of job enrichment, however, is that there must be some recognition of the meaningfulness of what people do. Therefore the experience you give requires thought – giving any kind of experience will not necessarily bring benefits.

Equal opportunities

In an ideal world we would have no need to examine equal opportunities. Many of you will work for voluntary organisations based upon spiritual or humanitarian beliefs, and we don't want to offend by suggesting that you look into issues of equality. On the other hand, we are all products of the society in which we live. When young we tend to formulate our belief systems on the predominant values surrounding us. It is likely, then, that many of us were brought up in an era when women were expected to stay at home to raise a family, when families consisted of two parents of opposite sex, where the inhabitants of our town or village were predominantly white, where disabled people tended to be isolated within institutions or their own homes. But much has changed, and society has not been universally comfortable with these changes. In considering equal opportunities we must, as managers, reflect on the issues in terms of our responsibilities as employers and service providers.

Equal opportunities provisions exist within certain legislation which may affect you in your organisation. Examples of relevant legislation are:

- The Race Relations Act 1976
- The Chronically Sick and Disabled Persons Act 1970
- The Sex Discrimination Acts 1975 and 1986
- The Children Act 1989
- The NHS and Community Care Act 1990

Note that local authority social services departments usually require voluntary agencies providing services, either under a service agreement or contract or when caring for vulnerable client groups such as children, people with mental health problems or learning disabilities and older people, to have an effective equal opportunities policy in operation.

Let us look at some examples of behaviour which would be considered to be unequal or discriminatory.

1 Gender

- unwanted or unwelcome physical contact of any form which is considered unacceptable by the other person
- sexually explicit, derogatory statements causing offence to the individual
- sexually discriminating remarks causing an individual to feel threatened, humiliated or patronised
- intentional sexual behaviour which interferes with the employee's job performance, undermines job security or creates a threatening or intimidating working environment.

2 **Race**
  ● victimisation of a person on account of their race
  ● derogatory verbal or physical treatment of a person on the basis of their physical appearance and/or cultural background
  ● racially discriminating remarks which cause the individual to feel threatened, humiliated or patronised
  ● racially motivated behaviour which interferes with an individual's ability to do their job or creates an intimidating working environment.

3 **Disability**

  ● victimisation of a person due to their disability
  ● jokes about, or at the expense of, an individual's disability or disabled group to which they belong
  ● name calling in respect of disabilities
  ● remarks of an abusive or unfavourable character about people with disabilities
  ● physical restrictions on access to opportunities, whether giving or receiving service.

4 **Sexuality**

  ● victimisation of a person because of their sexuality
  ● jokes about, or at the expense of, someone's sexuality or the sexual identity of the group to which they belong
  ● the use of homosexual or lesbian names or titles which offend and/or intimidate the individual
  ● the use of remarks, images or material relating to an individual's sexuality which are offensive or which cause the individual to be threatened or humiliated.

Exercise 5.6   Equal opportunities in your organisation

List a few examples where you think your organisation, by way of its culture, tradition, behaviour or physical environment, may not give equality of opportunity to paid staff, volunteers or customers. Refer back to the list above. These may be in areas of gender, race, religion, mental or physical disability or sexual orientation.

What did you come up with? As a manager you may ask what you can do to tackle the examples you identified or to improve your organisation's track record in respect of equal opportunities. This may be fairly easy to resolve if it is due to lack of thought but tremendously difficult to deal with if there are strong feelings, particularly amongst other managers. There are many ways you can influence change, not all of which require head-first, neck-on-the-block tactics. Some may be long-term approaches which require gentle persistence – a dripping tap approach. Your own lead, by personal example, is perhaps the simplest. We shall deal with managing change in more detail in Chapter 6.

In the meantime, let us look at one example: applying the principles of equal opportunities to recruitment. Consider what your organisation does in respect of the following equal opportunity recruitment principles:

1   Recruitment advertisements should contain an equal opportunities statement encouraging and welcoming all people whether men or women, members of minority racial groups, lesbian or gay and all age groups.
2   Application forms and supporting information should include an equal opportunities statement. They should not ask for such discriminatory information as marital status, children and so on.
3   In large organisations equal opportunities monitoring is good practice to identify whether their advertising is attracting a mix of ethnic groups. Where certain groups are underrepresented in your organisation you should consider the reasons for this and consider targeting your advertising.
4   People responsible for interviewing candidates should be aware of their obligations to ensure equality and, where possible, have training and personnel support in selection and equal opportunities procedures.

Opportunities for volunteers

The requirements of volunteers with special needs should be considered, the most obvious being physical access to a place of work via wheelchair ramps, wide doors and the like. However, other aspects should also be taken into consideration. Perhaps the provision of reserved vehicle parking spaces for volunteers with physical disabilities would help. Similarly, with a little forethought the adaptation or provision of equipment – for example, hand rails, telephone amplifying equipment or simply the height at which equipment and materials are placed – can enable a disabled person to make a significant contribution to the organisation.

Be open also to the opportunity that volunteers of different cultures, race or sexuality may wish to help with your wider objectives. Quite simply, you should be equally accepting of all help. Be aware that your own responses and reactions to people often act as much as a barrier to volunteering or paid employment as does the physical work environment.

Equal opportunities policy

An organisation's equal opportunities policy should set out its objectives in respect of an individual's rights to fair and equal services and opportunities. It should set the standard of conduct required of its employees or members and act to reassure individuals that they will be treated with equity. We give an example below.

Example: Anytown Luncheon Club – Equal Opportunities Statement

The Club's objective is to ensure that no member or service user receives less favourable treatment, directly or indirectly on the grounds of gender, age, disability, marital status, natural or ethnic origin, creed or religion, HIV antibody status, sexual orientation or any other form of unjustifiable discrimination.

Staff (paid and volunteers) will be required to attend appropriate training in the provision of equal opportunity-based services.

The Club reminds all staff that each individual has obligations not to discriminate against any person on the grounds mentioned above. All members are required to comply with this equal opportunities policy. Failure to do so may result in management action.

The Club will strive to meet any communication needs of service users.

The Club will modify equipment and install special aids where practicable. Where possible the premises will be adapted to meet the needs of disabled members.

Any member or service user having a complaint as to discrimination or victimisation should raise the matter with the Club Manager in the first instance.

This is a short summarised example of an equal opportunities policy and covers the immediate needs of the smaller organisation providing voluntary services. Obviously, larger organisations, particularly those which employ staff, may require a more detailed policy having regard to employment and equal opportunities legislation.

6 Volunteers in teams

As a manager you will be used to a fair proportion of your plans, ideas and suggestions not coming to fruition. Often they'll be going quite well and then seem to fail, get lost or be overturned by someone else. They may deserve this treatment, but you can better influence outcomes or implement change by getting volunteers working together in effective teams. In this chapter we look at effective teamwork – the example of inter-agency working being a challenging one – and also at managing change.

Many of the skills we examined in Chapter 5 will have a place in effective teamwork, since it is about working well not only with others as individuals but by bringing their combined strengths together constructively. It is managing the chemistry of the group that is the challenge. Perhaps the most appropriate analogy to the manager is the conductor of an orchestra. Each individual's performance may be fine as is your relationship with them. Put them together and minor differences may become major difficulties. In managing a team effectively you may have to bring consensus from conflict and results from resistance.

Effective teams

As a manager you are probably a member of several different teams or work groups and, with a little thought, you could probably identify what makes some teams more effective than others. Some you may have little control over, in terms of who leads the team, who the members are, what the task is and so forth. Here you can make effective contributions but may eventually become frustrated by the overall performance. We shall look here at teams, either semi-permanent groupings or those specifically put together for a task, which you have some influence over and the skills and issues you need to consider to help the team be effective. By effective we mean getting the task completed successfully without the loss of life or limb of any of the team members!

We shall divide effective team management into four areas for simplicity, but each is important all of the time:

1   choosing the right team
2   managing the task to be done
3   managing the way the team works
4   managing the relationship between the team and the other parts of the organisation.

Choosing the right team

Being an effective team first requires having people with the right mix of skills and abilities. Automatically we tend to select people for their specialist functions or expertise – their jobs within the department or organisation. We might need financial advice or a legal perspective or an expert on the environment or the elderly. But effectiveness is also influenced by the individual team members' team role characteristics. In 1981 Belbin first began to identify that team members could bring different contributions to a team, compared to their usual work role. These are described below.

Team role contributions (after Belbin)

1   **The Plant:** Creative, imaginative, unorthodox. Solves difficult problems.
2   **The Resource Investigator:** Extrovert, enthusiastic, communicative. Explores opportunities. Develops contracts.
3   **The Coordinator:** Mature, confident and trusting. A good chairman. Clarifies goals, promotes decision-making.
4   **The Shaper:** Dynamic, outgoing, highly strung. Challenges, pressurises, finds ways round obstacles.
5   **The Monitor Evaluator:** Sober, strategic and discerning. Sees all options. Judges accurately.
6   **The Teamworker:** Social, mild, perceptive and accommodating. Listens, builds, averts friction.
7   **The Implementer:** Disciplined, reliable, conservative and efficient. Turns ideas into practical actions.
8   **The Completer:** Painstaking, conscientious, anxious. Searches out errors and omissions. Delivers on time.

Given the above additional team role perspective you need, where possible, to choose a balance of people who can make these different contributions. In small teams the members may have to carry more than one role. You need to have a good idea which ones you yourself are good at, and it may also help to tell volunteers what you expect of them – for example, 'I'm hoping you'll be able to give me some good ideas on . . .' [Plant] or 'I'll need you to help me get this finished on time . . .' [Completer]. Imagine the problems you would have with too many Completers and no Plants.

The size of the team is another variable you should consider. Five to seven is optimal for keeping everyone involved. If you need to have larger teams to ensure skill or party representation then be aware that some individuals will be reluctant to contribute. Whether these are volunteers or not you need to structure meetings to bring out those views. When numbers reach around 20 it is much more common for attendance to fall. As raising the level of volunteer attendance is a particular issue, smaller teams will usually be preferable.

Most important to your consideration of forming an effective team will be its leadership. Again you do not have to assume that you have to lead a project team yourself. It may be just the kind of challenge a volunteer needs to increase their motivation or sense of belonging to the organisation. You can be in a group led by one of your volunteers if you make both of your roles clear, although groups with two leaders do less well than with one. You should be well placed to recognise and give a volunteer leader the support they need.

Managing the task to be carried out

An effective team needs to know what it has to achieve, why it is doing it and the timescale over which it has to be done. Each team member has to be clear about this. The team leader's task becomes self-evident in communicating this clearly to the group and ensuring understanding and commitment from the team. The leader should control progress and also ensure that the group reviews its progress regularly and learns from its experience, especially its successes. He or she will draw on many of the skills and ideas we have already covered in this book – purpose, planning, communication, motivation and so on.

Managing the way the team works

The team leader has to manage the processes that occur within the team. Tuckman (1965) found that teams develop through four stages to reach an effective teamworking (see Table 6.1).

Table 6.1 Tuckman's four stages of teamwork

Team stage	Team behaviour	Team leader actions
Forming	Polite, impersonal, formal, watchful, guarded.	Getting people talking, introducing each other, giving purpose to the group
Storming	Resisting involvement, arguing, opting out, feeling stuck.	Resolving conflicts openly, permitting differences, involving everyone, supporting individuals.
Norming	Getting organised, working together, setting ground rules and procedures.	Focusing group effort, giving feedback and encouragement, developing skills.
Performing	Reaching decisions, producing results, working closely and supportively, being resourceful and creative.	Giving support and encouragement, steering the group, reviewing progress, challenging the results, feeding in new ideas, standing back.

The team leader has to move the group skilfully through from storming to performing and keep it there. Different skills are needed at different stages as shown in the Table 6.1. The team leader has to create the working atmosphere for the team by demonstrating support for all the members, valuing all contributions and showing trust. These modelled behaviours encourage team members to do likewise. They are particularly important behaviour to demonstrate when volunteers are working in mixed groups with paid professionals. Volunteers need to be given the opportunity to develop the skills they have in this setting and to share their perspectives.

Finally, the leader has to know how to bring the team to a conclusion. Early on, the team needs to know the project's lifespan, how decisions will be made, the status of the work they are doing and so on. At the end the leader should praise the team and show gratitude. If anything, this is demonstrated in the medium term by what is done with the results.

Managing the relationship between the team and other parts of the organisation

As a manager you should empower a team not only within it, but also between it and the rest of the department or organisation. You will need to tell the rest that you have given a team a specific job to do and that you will value the results. This will be particularly important if the team is mainly volunteers since this demonstrates that you value them as much as the paid staff. Managing these communications is part of preparing the ground for success ahead of the team's results. It takes extra effort but is worth it. Doing nothing can sometimes be interpreted as preparing for failure or undermining the team's efforts. If the team is working on a long-term project, then releasing some interim results will be helpful in keeping people informed.

Inter-agency working

It is often the case now that, to meet people's complex needs for social care, a number of agencies or organisations have to work together to provide a complex support package. Inter-agency working is, of course, not a new phenomenon within the statutory care sector. Social workers, nurses, teachers and other care professionals have long contributed to multi-agency case conferences and caseworking to maximise the contribution each may make to the client, the emphasis being on teamwork.

More recent changes, many of which we referred to in Chapter 2, have meant that volunteers and voluntary care organisations are increasingly involved in the care and support of people in the community. As a result, volunteers will become part of the inter-agency team. Furthermore, there is a trend towards collaboration between voluntary organisations in the delivery of services. This may occur where no single agency has sufficient voluntary helpers to operate the service efficiently on its own and combines with others to undertake a project or staff a facility. We know of cases where premises are provided by one voluntary agency and the helpers by another.

At the first line manager level many of these decisions may be made for you as organisational policy. Some voluntary organisations have been concerned that the more recent market-oriented culture would seriously affect the long-standing cooperation that has existed between voluntary groups. In re-examining their role some have centred on core tasks to preserve the identity of their organisation. Others have adopted a needs approach based upon the philosophy that they exist to serve the community and address identified needs. As such, these have been willing to share the work with others. Whichever of these approaches your organisation takes, you are there to implement it on the ground and to support volunteers.

Potential conflicts in inter-agency working exist every bit as much between people at grassroots level as they do for managers. While senior managers may struggle with the complexities of agency budgets, service contracts and the like and attempt to establish *modus operandi* for their specific agency, the relationships at the 'sharp end' may frequently command a manager's more immediate attention.

Relationships between volunteers and paid professionals may not always be fruitful. Historically, some volunteers have distrusted the motives, if not the politics, of salaried workers. Equally, paid staff have been suspicious of the motives of volunteers and have had concerns about their perceived amateurism and unreliability.

We'd like to think now that each group recognises the demands placed upon them by rapid changes both in legislation and within society generally and respects the professionalism, training and commitment of their counter-parts. Staff within statutory agencies are now educated as to the role which volunteers play in the provision of many essential services and recognise, through increasing contact in the field, the training and commitment required to meet the obligations. Voluntary organisations can now partici-pate in social workers' training.

Let us now look at a case study where a voluntary organisation may work closely with a range of other services to meet an individual's needs.

Case study: Inter-agency working

Phil, an 80 year-old widower, lives alone in his two-bedroom bungalow. He has no close relatives. His neighbours are also elderly. Until recently Phil led a reasonably active life, spending most of his spare time in his garden and green-house. He exhibits competitively at local flower shows and keeps his neigh-bours supplied with vegetables from his garden. Some weeks ago he fell in his garden and broke his hip. He has just had a hip replacement operation at the local hospital and returned home. The following support has been arranged.

General practitioner
She visited Phil shortly after his discharge from hospital. As he has previously enjoyed good health she has only seen him twice for check-ups. She prescribed something to help him sleep and advised him on getting mobile again. She advised Phil that the district nurse would keep her informed of his progress and that she would see him again if required.

District nurse
He initially visited daily to change dressings, assist with dressing Phil and to help get him more mobile. He liaised with Social Services for the allocation of a home care assistant to help Phil with his social and domestic needs.

Home care assistant
She visits Phil twice a week. On Mondays she does some domestic work. On

Fridays she collects his pension and does some shopping. She always sits with him to talk and is concerned that he is becoming depressed and withdrawn. He has little interest in his previous hobbies and eats very little. She has found it necessary to discuss the matter with the home care organiser who has referred the matter to a social worker.

Social worker
He has visited Phil and is concerned about his state of mind. He attributes this to Phil's enforced change in lifestyle as a result of his reduced mobility. He has discussed with him the possibility of attending a club operated by the local branch of National Age Support, a voluntary organisation which employs staff and offers day care, companionship and a nourishing meal. He recognises that Anytown Carers, a local informal voluntary group could contribute greatly to Phil's improvement by befriending visits, assisting with shopping and so on. He believes that Phil's care and rehabilitation will involve a range of agencies working together as a team and that good communications will be essential. He contacts each individual who will be involved in Phil's care and invites them to a case conference.

A case conference may be called by any individual or agency involved in the care and support of an individual but is usually arranged by a representative of Health or Social Services. In Phil's case the people involved are Social Services (social worker and home care assistant), the general practitioner, district nurse, day centre organiser, the representatives of National Age Support and Anytown Carers, and possibly Housing and Social Security Benefits representatives.

Example: Phil's case conference – what should happen

The client, his partner if any or an advocate would be invited to attend, but in this case Phil has declined. The person calling the case conference will normally have spoken with individual participants prior to the meeting to identify the potential contribution of each agency.

The precise procedure may vary from case to case but generally the following pattern is followed.

1   The chairperson (usually, but not always, an agency manager) explains the reason and purpose of the meeting and asks those present to briefly introduce themselves, their agency and their role in relation to the case. It is usual to indicate the period of time available for discussion, as this helps participants focus on the essentials of the case.

2   The person responsible for calling the case conference, in this case the social worker, presents the client profile, case history and the factors which should be addressed at this meeting. While not prejudging the outcome of the meeting, an outline plan and care objectives will be discussed. In this case the areas which are likely to be addressed will be:

- *Health:* physical and mental, prognosis, rehabilitation, medication
- *Social care:* personal and domestic support
- *Finance:* social welfare benefits and grants
- *Housing:* home adaptations and grants
- *Day care:* occupation, leisure, transport and so on
- *Communication:* between agencies.

3   Those present are asked to contribute both generally and specifically to the discussion. The chairperson may call upon individuals to expand on some areas, encourage others to contribute and, if necessary, ensure that participants neither digress from the matter in hand nor dominate the meeting. Volunteers should be able to make suggestions here.

4   When all parties have contributed, a care plan will be agreed and agency role allocated. A key worker will be designated whose role will include:

- managing and disseminating information and ensuring that each person or agency is aware of the roles of others
- ensuring that the client is aware of, and is in agreement with, the plan
- monitoring the effectiveness of the plan and evaluating its delivery
- encouraging and supporting the team
- arranging ongoing case conferences.

5   Minutes of the meeting containing the care plan and agency roles will be circulated to all participants, including the client, as soon as possible after the meeting.

The success of the case conference relies upon each person recognising the contribution of others and, as with all successful communication, being willing to listen to their views without feeling challenged or threatened. The chairperson has to get the group performing as soon as possible, using the skills described above, so that the conference can result in a plan of action. Volunteers may need some preparation to enable them to present an argument or their observations in an objective, concise and well structured way. Volunteers or their manager should also be prepared to state the level of commitment they can make, possibly drawing on the assertiveness skills discussed in Chapter 4 (pages 55–56).

Introducing change successfully

Much of this book has been premised upon the fact that change is now a constant in life. Major changes are impacting on the voluntary sector, the pace of change is increasing and it needs to be managed. Put another way there are only two constants in life – death and taxation. Good managers are alert to change and implement necessary change successfully. We need to recognise that change can be planned or imposed but that, through planning imposed change proactively, we can often avoid or soften its effects.

In introducing change we often talk about three states:

1   *current state* – knowing where we are now
2   *future desired state* – knowing where we want to be
3   *transition state* – knowing how we are going to get from here to there.

Kurt Lewin, a psychologist, offers an approach to how to deal with each state (1951). He sees managing change as a process of unfreezing, changing and refreezing people's behaviour. We need change plans which will loosen up people's ideas, make them less rigid, show them new methods and support them in these.

In formulating plans it is helpful to examine reasons why people resist change, and these too can be related to the states listed above.

- *Current state*
  - The current state is too comfortable or secure for people to desire change.
  - They see no reason to change.
  - They see change as an attack on their current performance.

- *Future desired state*
  - The new goals or vision are not accepted.
  - The new state is poorly communicated.
  - The new state is unimportant to people involved.
  - They can't agree about what needs to be achieved.
  - They believe it might mean more work, loss of status, loss of friends and so on.
  - They fear failure in the new situation.

- *Transitional state*
  - They don't support the person/people leading the change.
  - They weren't involved in planning.
  - They think the timing is wrong.
  - They think a different approach to the change would be better.

Volunteers involved in change might have any of these objections. Already we have discussed the importance of clarifying the purpose of the organisation, using a vision, and improving communications and motivation. But in planning change you need to recognise that, in any group, there will be a range from those extremely favourable to those completely hostile. Each standpoint needs to be approached sensitively in a way that directly addresses their concerns. This may make any one plan inadequate.

Consider the following short case study about the WRVS.

Case study: 'WRVS volunteers divided by the push for profits' (condensed from *Daily Telegraph* report, 2.11.94)

The *Daily Telegraph* reported on how the drive to commercialise the Women's Royal Voluntary Service had divided the charity's 140000 members and alienated some of the elderly women volunteers. In an attempt to streamline its finances and enable it to compete with private companies for hospital trust and local authority contracts to run kiosks and meals on wheels it has:

- relaunched itself with a new slogan and logo
- swapped its staid green uniforms for sweatshirts
- reorganised its divisions
- appointed its first chief executive
- started to bring in new managers with a business background
- made some of its headquarters staff redundant
- recruited new staff with new skills in fundraising and computing.

The 'old guard' acknowledge that some change was necessary but maintain that it has been too radical and implemented too quickly. Many older members are saying that it is not the organisation they originally joined. The sacking of some staff have angered others and led to some resignations in protest.

'This is not the way that a caring organisation should behave,' said one volunteer with 30 years' service. 'They are destroying the goodwill of people like myself who have given our time and energy over the years.'

'The whole philosophy of the organisation is to put people first, but people now seem to matter less than profits,' said another.

The changes were sparked by a review of the WRVS in 1991 at the request of the Home Office. Membership has been steadily declining since the wartime peak of one million and the chief executive believes that the WRVS must cast off its 'twinset and pearls' image to attract corporate sponsors and commercial partnerships. He said that the membership had been fully consulted about the changes and that most have taken it extremely well.

The current state is fairly obvious, there is some indication of a future more desirable state and clearly not everyone is happy with the change methods. Below we indicate what the broad steps in a change plan need to be.

Example: Initiating change – the steps in a change plan

Since individuals do not accept or adopt changes instantly, they cannot be implemented in a single step. Those wishing to have changes adopted must follow a series of sequential steps that support and assist the individual adoption process.

1   *Exposure.* Let people know what the innovation or change is all about. The message should be clear, positive, brief, easy to understand and rewarding in some way. You want to generate interest and curiosity.
2   *Promotion.* Begin to encourage people to come to you for information and to talk with others. Group discussions should be encouraged to air doubts and particularly to mould positive attitudes and to emphasise benefits for individuals or groups.
3   *Demonstration.* Provide some practical demonstration of the change, preferably in the individual's own environment or in conditions that are natural and comfortable. Emphasise how it will help or benefit the individual.
4   *Hands-on training.* Provide the individual with the skills needed to implement the change and provide hands-on experience. The risk of failure is greatest in this step, and close positive support and encouragement is critical.
5   *Support.* As the individual begins to apply the change, difficulties will continue to emerge. Additional training and encouragement are important but the need will diminish as confidence is gained.
6   *Follow-up.* It is important to maintain regular follow-up on the changes for some period of time. Personal contact, reminders, questionnaires and small group sessions are all helpful. Marketing people call this post-purchase reinforcement.

Success in seeing through the plan will be dependent on achieving a critical mass of people wanting to change and in dealing with resistance. Remember that people who object perform a valuable buffer function – you may actually have a lousy idea! They also have a right to an opinion and they have feelings which you should respect. We suggest below some ways in which you may reduce or eliminate resistance.

Example: Some ways to reduce or eliminate resistance to change

1   Involve interested parties in contributing to the planning of change.

2   *Clearly* define the goals and objectives for the change.

3   Transmit the goals and objectives for the change *in written form* to all involved, to reduce misunderstanding.

4   Address the 'people needs' of those involved. Disrupt only what needs to be changed. Help people retain friendships, comfortable settings, and group norms wherever this is possible.

5   Have the group involved in *planning* the change *announce* the change.

6   Design flexibility into change. Phase the change, where possible, to allow for the completion of current efforts and the assimilation of new behaviours.

7   Design open sessions where those involved can air their feelings about the change.

8   Be open and honest. Don't pretend that negative aspects of the change don't exist. Don't try to manoeuvre employees or trick them (not at this moment or any other).

9   Do not leave openings for a return to the status quo. If you are not ready to commit yourselves to the change, don't announce it. Once you have made your decisions, do not waver. To do so is to encourage resistance.

10   Continually focus on the *positive* aspects of the change.

11   Look for areas of agreement between yourself and your opposition.

12   Do not attack; be reasoned and controlled while not abusing your opposition or those involved in the change.

13   Time the change – its planning process, announcements, and implementation – as well as possible.

14   Establish the parameters of the change and attempt to close off unwarranted fears that this change is an implication of future changes.

15   Attempt to design change to reverse as few rights, benefits and privileges of the people involved as possible.

16   Design adequate retraining and adjustment mechanisms into plans for change.

All the above will take time, and experienced managers will appreciate that successful change implementation takes many months or even years. You should spend time planning how to implement change before you initiate any plan. This time should be spent in estimating where and what resistance there will be and ways for reducing this. Be sure you can present the change clearly and with well-reasoned underlying arguments. Always be positive and receptive to opposition but try to work out in advance where you can modify the changes in response to real fears.

7 Attracting and keeping volunteers

The expansion of voluntary organisations, both large and small, has meant greater competition for the relatively small number of people who are prepared to give their time freely to help those in need. Potential volunteers can be quite discerning as to the work and type of organisation to which they will donate their time. It is important to create a good image at the outset.

How good do we look?

The first step in attracting new volunteers, and hopefully keeping them, requires us to look at ourselves, our organisation and structure from the perspective of the new entrant. What impression do we create by the environment in which we work? What sort of general image do we portray as an organisation? How do we measure up in terms of friendliness and welcoming newcomers?

Like it or not, first impressions persist. If we don't create a good one we will be wasting valuable resources in terms of time and money in trying to attract new members. Here are a few practical suggestions to consider with regard to improving your organisation's image.

1 **Premises.** Consider what your premises look like from outside. Do they appear inviting and well maintained? Is access easy? The external appearance should give the impression that your organisation takes some pride in its function and is welcoming to visitors.
2 **First impressions.** What impression do you think people get when they walk in off the street? The people staffing the reception area should have some training in customer care. Basic politeness and helpfulness goes a long way. The appearance of this public area is important too. A disarray of papers, coffee cups and old equipment and so on does not convey a

good impression. The organisation should appear organised and purposeful.

3 **Visual materials.** What about the visual materials your organisation uses? The posters, leaflets, headed notepaper and suchlike should all present a professional image. The use of poorly reproduced or faded photocopies looks particularly amateur and sloppy. Noticeboards should be well maintained and accessible for all to see.

4 **Advertising.** How and where do you advertise? You know your area; you know the image of local newspapers. One newspaper may have cheap advertising space but is it read by those you are trying to reach? Choose where you advertise to maintain or enhance the image you want to convey.

Some will feel that money spent on advertising is wasted money. Some will agree with the commercial maxim that you have to invest to progress. Some money wisely invested in reasonable quality communications can enhance your image and the returns that flow from it – both human and financial.

Attracting volunteers

There are a number of methods you might consider using to make that initial contact with potential volunteers:

- advertising in a local newspaper
- posters in public places – shops, supermarkets, libraries, health centres
- local radio appeals and promotions
- stalls at local fairs, fetes, shows
- leaflets in libraries, supermarkets
- organising your own event or attending a volunteer fair
- recruitment roadshows using either a vehicle, caravan or community halls.

Organising these events needs planning, which we've previously dealt with, and some need to be used in combination. For example, organising your own event involves advertising, using posters, local newspapers, local radio and so on. When you arrange public events you should choose an appropriate venue. In our experience a key issue is finding venues where there is good 'passing trade' – for example, shopping precincts, entrances to libraries, out-of-town shopping centres. It is no use saving money on a venue that people find inaccessible and inhospitable. You have no doubt seen many examples of this. It is disappointing to invest time and energy in what, but for a little forethought and a small degree of risk, might have proved a really successful recruiting event.

Always consider the six Ps when undertaking such events: *Planning, Preparation and Practice Prevents Poor Performance!*

Writing job descriptions

Job descriptions can have a number of advantages for voluntary organisations and volunteers. First, they help ensure consistency in care, service and approach to the client or task. They aid the overall monitoring of standards and quality. They are an indication to others that you take the work in which you are engaged seriously. Above all, they help the volunteer appreciate the expectations and parameters of their role. When used in conjunction with a contract and a quality training programme the volunteer can feel secure in the knowledge that they are valued, working safely, managed effectively and performing a defined role for the client group being served.

A volunteer's job description should not be overlong or unduly bureaucratic. It should address the key tasks concerned with the volunteer role. We provide an example below which you may be able to use in principle.

Example: Anytown Luncheon Club for Homeless People

The Club is held in St Philips Church Hall on three days a week – Mondays, Wednesdays and Fridays from 12 noon until 2 p.m. It seeks to provide a cooked meal to people who are homeless in Anytown.

1   Helpers will meet at St Philips at 10 a.m. to assist with the preparation of the meal and the dining area, assist with the serving of meals and befriending of those attending the Club and with washing up and cleaning the hall which should be completed by 3 p.m.
2   Helpers who cannot attend on the day should contact the organiser by telephone as soon as possible and no later than 9 a.m. on the day.
3   In the interests of Health and Safety and the conditions of hire of the hall no smoking is permitted by helpers at any time.
4   Helpers agree to attend the food handling and preparation course operated by the Environmental Health Department as soon as possible after joining the Club and to comply with the appropriate regulations.
5   Helpers will read and comply with the published fire regulations and ensure that all fire exits remain free of obstruction.
6   All helpers and client attendances, accidents or untoward occurrences must be recorded in the day book.
7   All services of the Club are provided within St Philips Church Hall. Helpers should not undertake duties outside of the Club's hours or premises. Where

a client requires additional support the helper should discuss the need with the organiser or senior person in attendance who will contact the appropriate agency as necessary.

8   Claims for reimbursement of expenses must be submitted by the end of each month to the organiser.

This job description has been kept to one page and addresses the key tasks and safety aspects, both personal and environmental, associated with the club. It covers the times and places of duty and what the volunteer should do if unable to attend. It identifies the rules and regulations required of validating agencies governing the operation of the club. The safety of helpers is addressed both in the statutory requirements of Health and Safety and Fire but also in regard to not undertaking work outside of the club. The training obligations are unambiguously stated as is the date of expense claims. This example is intended as a guide, and you will have to think through the issues when applying it in your own organisation – notably whether it is ready for this. A clear job description not only helps avoid disagreement but, if updated regularly, can assist in the monitoring of the service which you are providing.

Making 'safe' appointments

Making safe appointments is important for several reasons: to safeguard the organisation's reputation; to protect the interests and integrity of other volunteers; and ultimately to ensure the safety of those whom we exist to serve.

One area of concern is the apparently growing number of people in society prepared to take advantage of the vulnerable people whom many voluntary groups exist to help. It is now routine within the statutory care sector for those who work with children, the elderly, the disabled and with other vulnerable people to be subject to police checks. We will all be able to recall media reports of people who have abused trusted positions or who have presented themselves fraudulently to obtain advantage of such groups.

This is a difficult area to handle. We find that many voluntary groups take the view that people who offer help are to be trusted solely because of their offer of help. One potential effect of the statutory sector strengthening its gatekeeping practices may be that some displaced persons will seek access to vulnerable people through the offices of a charity.

A more widespread reason for introducing sound recruiting practices for volunteers is that people may choose voluntary work for the wrong reasons or at the wrong time. Some see it as a way of working through their own difficulties at a time when they are struggling themselves with a difficult problem

– commonly following a bereavement or a divorce. When a person is under-going considerable stress or emotional difficulties voluntary work may not be the best therapy. You may need to ask whether they are really ready or advise that they defer their intention to volunteer until such time as they have resolved their own difficulties. Alternatively there may be some helping activities which don't involve direct client contact which both of you will agree on.

There is no guaranteed 'safe' way of making appointments, but the process should ideally include the following: application form, references, declar-ation as to any convictions, interview and, where the person will work with vulnerable people, a request to social services for a police check. We cover each of these in turn below.

The application form

This need not be unduly lengthy and one should always be mindful of the need to file and retain the information and obtain easy access. Do remember that the Data Protection Act applies to all computer-held records.

Basic information should include the candidate's personal details: full name, age, address, date of birth and occupation. Details of relevant employ-ment experience and previous voluntary experience is helpful in identifying an individual's potential as is a space asking the individual to indicate what they have to offer the organisation. Ensure also that there is a clearly defined space to write the names of two referees.

References

As discussed above, while these are not guaranteed to ensure that the person appointed is safe, they do provide a measure of security both as an initial gatekeeping mechanism to persons intending to exploit the voluntary organisation and with regard to the information obtained from referees. References also act as a mark of security for clients using the organisation's services.

A standard letter bearing the organisation's letterhead may be prepared for referees, indicating that the applicant is seeking to do voluntary work. The type of work should be stated – for example, fundraiser, collector, home visitor, escort car driver. The reference may be given in letter format or by means of a form asking questions. A request for information as to whether the person is known to have any criminal convictions or serious health diffi-culties should be included. It is important to emphasise that the information contained in the reference will be treated confidentially. A stamped addressed envelope for returning the completed reference should be enclosed with the request.

Declaration of convictions

The Children Act 1989 requires those who work with children to be subject to checks as to their suitability. A wise organisation will offer the same safeguards to other vulnerable members of society, such as the elderly and people with learning disabilities.

The Magistrates Courts Act 1980 permits individuals who have been convicted of offences to consider their convictions 'spent' after a certain number of years. They do not therefore have to disclose their history to employers. The number of years is set by statute in relation to the severity of the offence. Where volunteers are likely to be working with vulnerable client groups, especially children, it would be wise to require a declaration of all past offences. In statutory organisations these are always required to be disclosed. The Children Act provides for this disclosure.

The decision whether to appoint a person who has previously committed a criminal offence to a voluntary position is solely that of the voluntary organisation who will consider the safety of the clients, other volunteers, the reputation of the organisation and so on. We would expect that the organisation would also consider the individual potential volunteer. A reasonable judgement needs to be made based on how long it is since the person 'sinned', how old they were, the nature of the offence, the circumstances, the likelihood of a recurrence, what their references say now, whether voluntary work will help the person and allow them to help others. There can be many roles in voluntary organisations which do not involve direct care roles or the handling of money.

As with references, information concerning previous convictions should be treated in the strictest confidence and not disclosed to others.

The interview

The interview is more an informal meeting of the applicant, an experienced person in a senior position, such as a branch manager or local organiser, and the person who is likely to be working closely with the new volunteer. An informal atmosphere is essential as you will want to learn as much about the person as possible and you will wish for them to learn as much as possible about you and your organisation.

Your objectives for the meeting should include:

- introducing the organisation, its philosophy and practice
- finding out what they want to gain from voluntary work
- talking through the variety of activities they could undertake
- identifying any special skills they may have
- clarifying their commitment and availability

- identifying any actual/potential training needs
- examining the opportunities for a volunteer contract of attendance.

Before the interview you should have already sent them some literature about your group and will have perhaps had a chat on the telephone. You should have received their application form, replies to reference requests and had good time to consider the role(s) the person could play in your work. It is wise to set a time limit for the meeting which really should not exceed an hour at the most.

Although you intend to be informal and the person is giving their time freely to meet with you and offer help, they will still feel a degree of apprehension at meeting you for the first time. Be aware of this and try to put them at ease. Explain the purpose of the meeting and why it was necessary to obtain references. If these are in order tell them so. Remember that it is best to ask open questions such as 'How would you like to help us?' rather than closed questions such as 'Would you like to help with our flag week?'. A good rule in any helping situation or interview is to try to listen for two-thirds of the time and speak for only one-third. This ensures that the other person has the opportunity to ask all their questions and allows you to elicit information.

It is good preparation before the interview to write down the themes you wish to be raised and some examples of questions designed to obtain information about these. You can share these between yourself and the other interviewer. In the interview, when you think you have covered all the points, summarise what you have agreed together. You should then discuss a written agreement (contract) which confirms what the organisation expects of the volunteer and what in return it will offer in terms of support and training. This will normally include a review process after an initial settling-in period.

Using contracts

The idea of using contracts with people who give their time freely may, at first sight, cause you some apprehension. Most of us have had experience of contracts within our paid working life and may feel that they equate with discipline, rigidity, inflexibility and bureaucracy. On the other hand, we may see a contract as offering security, clarifying our conditions of service, ensuring our safety and, in some cases, ensuring that an employer does not exploit us.

Most people who give voluntary time already accept the concept of an informal contract which entails turning up to help on a regular basis, often on a certain day at a given time. There will be an informal code of conduct with regard to dress, attitudes and behaviour while engaged in the work. Those who work with people, directly or indirectly, will accept the need for confidentiality both in respect of clients and colleagues with whom they work. Given this you may ask what the need is for a written contract. Our answer would be that it is a very helpful aid to learning what is expected of you when you first become a volunteer in your organisation.

Exercise 7.1   Conveying expectations

Think about the ways in which the expectations of a volunteer's job in your organisation are made known to new volunteers.
    Are these

- written down?
- passed on by long serving members?
- part of a structured training programme?

    Can you remember ever being uncertain as to what was expected of you as a new volunteer? How did this make you feel?

Many organisations still leave people to discover some of the vital aspects of their job by chance. Worse still, they sometimes only find what they *should* be doing when they've done something wrong. In the case of a volunteer, you can imagine that this could be traumatic and possibly result in losing the individual's services. Although it is impossible to pass on everything at a first meeting, or to write guidance on every eventuality, an individual volunteer contract can offer a sense of direction and security to the volunteer, the manager and, ultimately, to the group of people whom you are serving.
    Let us look at a case study.

Case study: Phil – the potential volunteer

Phil would like to be described as young middle-aged; he is in full-time employment and has rather demanding family commitments. He has responded to a local advertisement for volunteers to assist people with mobility difficulties when they visit the local town centre. Every Saturday during term-time Phil goes to town because his daughter attends her ballet class there.
    Phil would like to help but is worried he may be unable to attend on any given day. He has also heard from friends that, once the organisation recruits you as a volunteer, it will require more and more of your time. And, of course, he would like to know a bit more about the type of person he would be helping and how he could best assist.

The following is an example of a simple one-page contract which clarifies the basic situation between the organisation and the volunteer. More elaborate formats are used by some organisations but we believe that it is best to keep the form simple and to ensure that the contract does not solely favour the organisation.

Example: Anytown Shopping Mobility Group – volunteer contract

Name of Volunteer: Phil McSweeney   Name of Organiser: Betty Smith
                                      Telephone: Anytown 54321

                                      Personal Contact: Bill Brent
                                      Telephone: Anytown 54322

Anytown Shopping Mobility Group assists people with mobility difficulties as a result of age, physical or sensory disability to undertake personal shopping within Anytown Town Centre.

The group has the use of a large private car park adjacent to their offices and with easy access to the town centre where, for a small charge, clients may park while shopping. The group assists users by loaning wheelchairs and other walking aids and by assisting with the pushing of wheelchairs and escorting people with sensory or walking difficulties around the town.

An indemnity insurance ensures that all helpers are insured against personal and third-party risks while performing their duties with the group.

New volunteer helpers are required to attend an introductory day where both professionally qualified and experienced facilitators will, through the use of talks and practical exercises, share knowledge of disabling conditions and demonstrate safe ways of assisting people with disabilities.

Regular monthly meetings are held on the second Tuesday of each month at 8 p.m. in the office where talks are given on topical issues followed by a social event. Helpers are invited to attend these meetings, accompanied by family or friends.

During the introduction day and the following four occasions when you give help you will be paired with a mentor who is an experienced volunteer like yourself. He/she will answer any questions which you may have regarding the group or its work. Your mentor is available to speak with you on the telephone at any time on matters relating to your voluntary duties.

The date of your introductory day is Saturday _____ and your mentor is Bill Brent.

You have undertaken to be available on Saturday mornings from 9.30 until 12.30.

In the event of you being unable to attend, you will notify the office as soon as possible.

While acting as a helper, you will be expected to comply with the written policies of the group relating to Equal Opportunities, Health and Safety, Smoking and confidentiality of information. On completing the introductory day and four sessions, helpers are offered the opportunity to discuss their experience and any needs which they may have with the organiser and their mentor.

Signed: _____ P. McSweeney   _____ Betty Smith

The above specimen contract simply identifies the basic needs of the organisation in relation to training, attendance, legal liabilities, and philosophy. Equally, the volunteer is assured that he will be trained in the first instance, and offered ongoing support and further training should he need it. He knows that he is insured should an accident occur either to himself or to someone he is helping. There is a named contact person in addition to the 'boss' to whom he may turn for guidance. There is leeway in respect of the time allocated to reduce any time pressures on Phil, and he knows that he can excuse himself should he face other demands but is expected to advise the organisation. Importantly, for both the organisation and the volunteer, there is a set time at which both may assess their compatibility, and the opportunity to discuss this is built into the original agreement.

Keeping volunteers

We reiterate that volunteers are one of a voluntary organisation's most prized resources. Without them we cannot provide the services we promise our users. We need to keep volunteers not only to achieve our purpose but also because of the investment we have made in terms of recruitment and training costs. Once trained, volunteers not only represent good value for money within an organisation into which money may be difficult to attract, they are also a prime source of recruiting other volunteers through their wide networks of friends and acquaintances.

There are a number of principles we can apply to keeping volunteers, many of which we have referred to earlier, particularly in Chapters 5 and 6. We will be more successful if we have a good understanding of why each has volunteered and what motivates them. We need to be aware of the principles of job design and giving experience as part of keeping volunteers stimulated. Several times we have mentioned the importance of good two-way communication and keeping in touch with volunteers.

We would draw attention to the importance of the following issues:

- **Training.** Specific training should be provided for the role to be performed as well as a sound general induction programme to your organisation. Induction should cover the wider structure and aims of the organisation so that the volunteer can see the context of their contribution. It should also cover issues such as how they can access a grievance procedure if they wish to pursue particular problems 'formally' with their manager. How the organisation adheres to relevant legislation to create a safe working environment, as well as observance of equal opportunities (discussed in Chapter 5) and good standards of confidentiality practice, should also be covered. As a manager you have an important role in ensuring that what is set out at induction is what actually happens.
- **Supervision.** Good quality supervision should be provided by persons who possess both sound management skills in addition to practical experience.
- **Flexibility.** Flexibility is required in respect of the volunteer's contribution and role. An individual's availability for voluntary work may change in response to their other commitments, whether family, work or social demands. The forward-thinking organisation and manager must recognise this and be both sympathetic and responsive. You should be prepared to allow 'time out' for a specified period of time, or a reduction in hours or even job-sharing, without detriment where possible to the volunteer's usual role and responsibilities. Alternatively, a positive outcome may be achieved by the volunteer agreeing to a planned programme of change to obtain new experience or work with new people in the organisation. The opportunity to enable other volunteers to gain experience of a different area of work during a volunteer's absence should also be considered.
- **Follow-up.** There should be a deliberate policy of following up volunteers who do not attend for a period of time. You should ensure that contact is made as soon as it is evident that a volunteer has not attended for a specified period. You need to deal with the situation with tact and privacy, since an individual may have particular difficulties involving family, work or other relationships. However, some support during a period of temporary difficulty may ensure that the volunteer will later return to making a valuable contribution. A personal visit, rather than a letter or telephone call, will demonstrate your concern more readily as well as give you better opportunity to identify reasons for the volunteer's absence.

The volunteer contract above mentions the role of the mentor, a named person who acts as an experienced guide or friend the volunteer can talk to. Where possible, this should be an informal arrangement struck between the volunteer and a manager who doesn't directly manage the volunteer. This is often found to be a valuable support mechanism for volunteers not only to resolve immediate problems but to provide long-term support, career guidance or counselling. It should not be forced on either the volunteer or manager; it is just a useful option.

The mentor relationship does not preclude you, as a manager, from giving the volunteer necessary supervision, support and coaching. We would reiterate some key components to supporting individual volunteers – finding time, good communication, listening, setting objectives and so on. One aspect to communication which is often overlooked is access to circulated written information that passes between managers. Internal newsletters, noticeboards, and adequate copying facilities will help here.

We mentioned earlier the use of an exit interview to find out why volunteers leave. If you are losing a number of volunteers it is worth looking into what your organisation is doing to them rather than attributing it to personal reasons. This enquiry may be conducted by telephone, and you should ask whether the organisation has been sufficiently supportive or whether there is anything you could have done that would have improved matters. You may receive some unpleasant feedback that indicates change is needed. Remember to make all possible efforts to keep those people in whom you have invested. You can't afford to keep losing them.

8 Delighting the customer

First and last, voluntary organisations are there to help their 'customers'. We all know this, we hear you saying. If this is so obvious then why are we saying it? That we are sometimes at risk of forgetting this is perhaps putting it too strongly, but do we sometimes forget to show our customers that we believe it? You only have to spend a day shopping to know that good quality service is not everyone's top priority. Sometimes we can let all the other priorities we have acquired crowd out the customer. Sometimes we say we'll call someone back with an answer and forget until the next day. Does the telephone ring twelve times while we're talking about our holiday? Do we *always* put our customers first?

This chapter is about quality – about what delivering quality really implies in practice. The title of the chapter has been chosen deliberately since most recent definitions of quality centre on delighting the customer or exceeding customer expectations. It recognises that we can't always give a five-star service, but that isn't expected. Customers hoping for a lift to the chemist to exchange their prescriptions don't expect a Rolls Royce Silver Shadow. A two-door saloon will do. But being given a definite pick-up time might exceed their expectations. In considering quality we also have to think about how to give the best quality service within the resources available to us.

Growing expectations

You might be happier with another term instead of 'customer'. 'Client' is the most favoured term in the voluntary sector. We don't believe that the semantics are particularly important; we need only agree on how to refer to the recipients of our services. What is important is that consumer expectation of the quality of *all* services received is growing. The public more readily complain when they are dissatisfied with services. For example, the number of

NHS complaints rose by over 50 per cent from 1991–92 to 1993–94. This is not thought to be a particular reflection of declining quality of service, but more a readiness to complain.

The 'consumer industry' is growing apace too. Rising numbers of complaints about all public services are largely assumed to be due to consumers feeling more empowered by the Citizen's Charter initiative. Increasing numbers of service organisations have developed their own charters too. General practitioners are now being encouraged to develop their own practice charters. For many of these services the public are also supported by detailed information on how to complain and, ultimately, by an ombudsman. Again in the NHS there is a major complaints review underway to simplify the process for patients in making complaints and to improve the service's responsiveness. From April 1996 onwards local councils will be expected to produce community care charters, setting out the standards of community care services people can expect.

Another rapidly developing branch of the 'industry' is the production of league tables. These are designed to give people comparative information about performance against selected standards, the purpose being to empower the consumer to make informed choices. So far, national examples for education and health have been published.

Much of this activity is driven by government policy and may be tarnished with the brush of political expediency. Critics see the league tables as either crude or not consumer-driven – that is, not necessarily what consumers have identified that they want. The education league tables make no allowances for variable 'inputs', for example, by not accepting that children start off with different degrees of advantage. The health league tables have been criticised for giving no information about clinical outcomes, mostly being oriented towards waiting times. However, the government continues to restate its commitment to making public services more responsive and accountable, and it is likely the methods will become more valid and acceptable over time.

The quality imperative

In the commercial world the importance of delivering quality services and products is accepted worldwide as a fundamental prerequisite to competing in a competitive environment. It is not a choice. In the public sector there appears to be a political will to create more consumerism and improve standards of public service. The message for the voluntary sector must be that it cannot ignore these trends towards empowering the average consumer to demand improved services and exercise their rights to get them. If part of your organisation's remit is to bring pressure to bear on government or service providers then you will welcome this. If you actually provide services or advice directly then you cannot rely on assumptions that 'We've always been consumer oriented' or that people will continue to be eternally grateful for a service that is merely adequate.

We shall try to explain some of the reasons for our thinking in this area and show why we believe customer service in the voluntary sector needs to continually improve. First, consider what would happen if this pressure on the statutory services actually starts to work? Ordinary people become more empowered and begin to receive more of the services they need, or at least begin to obtain more articulate explanations for the shortfall. If the voluntary sector didn't keep pace would that start to undermine the need for the voluntary sector? Whilst this might be fanciful, the failure of voluntary services to continue to appear more responsive will erode the goodwill it earns from many who donate to it.

Second, we need to consider the effects of competition. Health care reforms have created an internal market in health care delivery much like the real market in elderly residential care that exists in the independent sector. In theory this competition will drive down prices and at the same time improve the quality of services. This may be no threat to the voluntary sector as a whole, but an increasing contract culture will squeeze many voluntary organisations. Assume that, as a purchaser of services, we wanted to contract for a voluntary organisation to provide us with an independent advocacy service, or a transport service for elderly clients to and from a day centre. Although there are several voluntary organisations we might approach to meet our needs we would have to establish that the organisation can provide a consistently high quality service. Is your organisation ready for this?

Third, we should examine some of the quality issues surrounding fundraising. Some organisations handle it all centrally, in others local managers and volunteers may play a large part. How much of what is donated to your organisation comes directly or indirectly from people who have received services from it? It is likely that their willingness to give will be coloured by their perception of the quality of service you give. Other donors will want to be convinced that you use the money effectively – another component of quality.

Larger charities are increasingly recognising that they have to portray a high quality image. This is important for both direct fundraising and trading-based organisations. No one examining the National Trust's merchandising standards would doubt the importance they attribute to quality.

Our concerns are that poor quality service or image will erode the voluntary sector's funding base. At the same time statutory services may improve for those able to exercise their rights, but there will always be those less advantaged who will need your help.

A theory from the advertising world says that when anyone receives a good service they tell three people about it on average. But when they receive a bad service they tell 20 people. On that calculation poor quality companies have to find seven times as many customers as good companies to keep pace with them, or alternatively they can choose to go out of business. Mercenary though it may sound there is a market share of donations to be 'won'. This is influenced by the consistent quality of service the organisation gives. Every member of that organisation from the chairman to the volunteer acts as an ambassador for it, regardless of whether they're off the job or on it. Put another way, the public views each voluntary organisation as a 'brand' name, and brands have to be built by reputation. Managers need to convince volunteers of the importance of this aspect of their role – their behaviour makes a statement about the organisation. Since the mid-1980s total voluntary giving in real terms has remained virtually static. In 1994 the largest 200 charities saw their income rise by 4 per cent. The remainder suffered a decline, and that gap is growing.

Quality matters not just because of the intrinsic value of providing someone with a service they need but because of the contribution it makes to your organisation's ability to continue doing what it believes in. Everybody you provide a service to will potentially want to thank you in the way they know how – by making a donation.

Quality? How do you 'do' it?

This question is sometimes met with a 'You tell me and we'll both know' sort of answer. Quality has its gurus and its converts but if you are in an organisation with a demonstrable commitment to quality, supported by a working strategy, you are probably in a lucky minority. All quality gurus are united in the view that the only meaningful definition of quality is the *customer's perception of quality*.

As indicated above, the driving force for quality in the private sector has been the competitive environment; quality has been about winning customer loyalty through continuing quality of service. In the public sector there may be increasing elements of this ethos, but the driving forces have been more oriented towards winning business in the internal market and demonstrating accountability to the public. We have suggested that the voluntary sector needs to pay attention to delivering a quality service both because of a potentially growing 'market' and to maintain its goodwill among the public.

Two similar approaches to quality have emerged strongly in the last decade or so – Total Quality Management (TQM) and Continuous Quality Improvement (CQI). Deming (1986), a founding father of the quality movement, and most other quality gurus agree that the best definition of TQM is 'to do the right thing right the first time, on time, all the time, and to strive always for improvement and customer satisfaction'. Both TQM and CQI set us some guiding values to any quality strategy we might consider. We shall address some of these basic values and then share a couple of quality techniques you might find useful at work.

Let's start by asking you a couple of questions about quality in your organisation.

Exercise 8.1   Quality in your organisation

Have you ever considered how well your organisation provides a quality service to its customers? If you could imagine yourself in the 'shoes' of your customers asking for services from you, what would you say are the strengths of your organisation or branch? List these strengths.

Conversely, what would you say are its main weaknesses? List these weaknesses.

You should have been able to list some of each – hopefully more strengths than weaknesses. To achieve a high quality service these weaknesses will have to be eliminated.

Oakland (1989) has identified some commonly occurring weaknesses in organisations:

- **Not changing.** You do what you've always done, or expect things to get better when you haven't changed the way you do anything.
- **Compartmentalisation.** Each department or function works for itself, failing to recognise or heed the needs or expectations of others – their internal customers. This results in you having to do the work you can't get others to do before you can get on with your own work.
- **The 'Acceptable Quality Level' (AQL).** This means the level of errors or defects regarded as inevitable. When we assume errors are inevitable we stop trying to prevent them occurring. We look for errors after we have done the work – detection – rather than trying to stop them occurring in the first place – prevention. Crosby, another quality guru, author of *Quality is Free* (1979), believes that it is not quality that costs but 'unquality', the costs associated with continuously putting things right. This cost in organisations is often put at between 20–40 per cent of operating costs.
- **Firefighting.** Firefighting is macho! What a busy day some managers have solving all those problems that seem to come out of nowhere. With a little forethought how many of them would never have arisen? In one major UK service organisation it was calculated that the level of firefighting – doing extra work to 'fix' problems – was 2.5 hours per person per day.

- **The 'not my problem' syndrome.** Two-thirds of all problems arise at a different point from where they were caused and are left to be resolved by different people. Can we eliminate these problems at source instead of exporting them to other people all the time?

How many of these weaknesses exist in your organisation? Are there any plans to introduce quality initiatives? As many organisations fail in their attempts to implement quality as succeed.

Key factors in successful implementation are:

- drive and commitment from the top down
- commitment to ownership and participation from all staff
- clear organisational purpose, objectives and so on
- systematic ways of identifying quality problems
- clear quality methods to address identified problems
- performance monitoring and sharing of results
- feedback mechanisms both internally and from customers to evaluate improvement
- recognition of individual contributions and responsibilities
- appropriate appraisal methods, training, support and individual development
- signing up to a long-term commitment.

This appears a daunting list but, in our view, none can be dispensed with. Some are easier to put in place than others but probably the most difficult problem to contend with is lack of commitment from above. You are part of that commitment for those staff and volunteers working for you. For your volunteers quality begins with you. If you want them to improve they will need your lead.

The long-term commitment issue is also another difficult area. We meet some people who think they've implemented quality in their organisation by instituting a suggestion box scheme, or a complaints procedure, or by raising the subject occasionally at a team meeting. Our view is usually that they've sprinted the first hundred yards of what is actually a marathon. You need to convey the need for long-term commitment to quality to volunteers too.

There is a further challenge in helping volunteers come to terms with all these quality ideas – to do it without making them feel defensive about what they've always been doing. Raising the quality spectre is often perceived as a challenge to people's esteem for their current performance. From the list above we're going to address three clear and practical quality methods which will help you work through quality implementation with volunteers. These are:

- quality chains
- quality improvement teams
- seeking feedback.

Quality chains

The idea of quality chains simply is that, throughout all organisations, there are a series of links from the input end to the output end. People telephoning your organisation for advice could be perceived as arriving at the 'input' end. They may be advised on the telephone to come in and see someone by appointment. When they've been seen they may be passed to someone else for more specialised advice. When they've got the information they want they leave at the 'output' end after taking part in a number of 'processes'. To fully meet customers' requirements, and therefore to give a quality service, the chain of services along which they are passed must not be broken.

You need to ask some questions about the quality of service given in this chain. First, how efficiently are customers passed along the quality chain – for example, are the hold-ups due to someone being unable to make an appointment or no one knowing where the person they want to see is? Second, is the link person at each stage of the chain making a positive contribution to what that customer needs? In quality terms we would call this 'added value'. Do you know what value is being added to the outcome for each customer by each contact they have along the quality chain? Is the service you give, and particularly that being given by volunteers, effective? Are there any unnecessary links in the chain?

These two ideas, the quality chain and added value, are considered cornerstones in total quality management thinking. A third is the focus on internal customers. The idea here is that, in a chain, everyone receives a service from someone as a customer and supplies a service to someone else, becoming a supplier. That person takes on responsibility for managing quality in the chain at that time and for not exporting their poor quality further along the chain. Simple examples might be giving clear messages on the telephone about a planned home visit or accurately recording an appointment time in the diary. Do you ever find yourself having to apologise to your contacts for the mistakes others have made in your chain? Failures in these internal customer links almost always find their way to the interface between the organisation and the customer.

You can make improvements to these chain reactions. Persuading your team that they are a valuable link in a chain and not working in isolation will help. Helping volunteers to see the ramifications of their actions later in the chain – that they're exporting their quality problems – may also be helpful. Ask them some simple questions about their place in the chain process. Ask them if they get good quality service from their supplier? Have you given the best service to your customer before passing them on to the next link? How do you know you're delivering the best service? What are you doing about the problems you've identified?

Quality improvement teams

This idea originates from Japan. You may be more familiar with a similar idea called quality circles. We shall describe both of these. Quality circles are groups of workers given the remit by management to meet fairly regularly to identify quality problems and their possible solutions. These solutions are usually forwarded to management and, if the concept of the circle is to work, management has to be receptive to the suggestions proposed. Some will be 'free' and some will have resource implications. Circles usually have a long life, working through one quality issue to the next. The meetings are not led by managers nor do managers attend them. The group motivates itself by improving its own working arrangements and by being given recognition by management.

Some view quality circles and quality improvement teams as synonymous. Organisations sometimes have quality action teams too! However, we shall describe quality improvement teams as being different to quality circles. They usually have a short life, being targeted to find and implement a solution to a particular quality problem, resolve it and then disband. They are put together by, and report back to, management. They should comprise members of all the different specialities or groups with an interest in improving the matter in hand. They may include both workers and managers, and this diversified membership brings different perspectives to the problem. They are sometimes referred to as 'cross-functional teams'.

In the voluntary sector you may have spotted applications for both type of teams described. You may even think you have similar teams in existence already working on quality issues. Whichever type you favour there is a place for the volunteer in both. Quality circles could be almost entirely composed of, and even led by, volunteers. Quality improvement teams could have volunteer members to contribute their perspective, and this would certainly be of value to both parties. You may need to offer volunteers your support in either role.

Seeking feedback

If we accept that, in trying to define a quality service, we must take account of the customer's perspective we must identify ways in which we can find out from our customers whether what we offer is meeting their needs. There are a great many ways of doing this, from the simple to the complex. Our first rule would be to match the investment in time and resource to the possible outcome gains. To be pragmatic, we should not invest a great deal of time and money in, for example, an extensive postal survey to find out if people read our new sign on the front door. On the other hand, we can underinvest in finding out about really important aspects of our service.

Of the ways indicated above, perhaps one with which most people are familiar is the brief satisfaction questionnaire often found in restaurants and hotel rooms. It may ask four or five key questions about aspects of the service and how satisfied you were with them. Usually the questions have an answer scale rather than 'yes/no' or 'agree/disagree' since these leave no opportunity to measure shades of opinion. People are rarely totally satisfied or totally dissatisfied, but given only two options you force them to pick one and probably obtain deceptive results. Here is an example.

Example: Satisfaction questionnaire

	Always Pleased	Often Pleased	Sometimes Displeased	Always Displeased
How do you feel about the meals we deliver to you?				
How pleased are you by the meals we deliver you?				

You may think both questions are exactly the same. Essentially they are, but the first puts the question in a fair way whereas the second introduces a bias – you are conveying that you expect the respondent to answer that they *are* pleased. Although providing four options gives a choice, there is deliberately no neutral choice so that respondents cannot 'sit on the fence'.

Rating scales can be of various types; another common method is to use numbers from, say, 1 to 6. Yet measuring satisfaction may not, in itself, always be useful. You may gain better information by asking questions about standards – for example, how hot the food is, how well presented it is, whether it arrives on time and so on. You may also want to invite comment about areas of dissatisfaction or suggestions for improvement. Often we have found that when people are asked what they found unsatisfactory about a service they will say they are quite happy but will offer improvement suggestions if asked.

If you want questionnaires to be returned by post you will improve response rates by including stamped addressed envelopes. You can also use this questionnaire approach in street interviews, by telephone survey or organise other collection methods such as suggestion boxes. Remember to allow time for analysis and don't make your questionnaire too complicated, especially if you can't operate a computer spreadsheet.

There are other ways of seeking feedback, some of which are much more informal. In your day-to-day dealings with people you can ask them what they think of the service you provide. You can ask volunteers to do this and pool your findings at team meetings. You can formalise this into a few interview topics or actual questions which you can ask individual customers. One useful way of obtaining rapid relevant feedback is from a focus group – a joint meeting of several of your customers to whom you put a range of questions for their collective feedback.

While much of this sounds straightforward there are some important elements to remember. First you must have ground rules for confidentiality and anonymity. Some people may not mind discussing a quality problem with you, but it may involve another volunteer or paid carer and create risks for the customer. You must establish with the respondent that they can give feedback confidentially and that, while you may know who they are, no one else will. If you involve volunteers in collecting feedback in this way they too must respect confidential information. Replies to postal questionnaires can be anonymous; no one should know who sent them.

Finally we have to say that we have encountered managers in the voluntary sector who aren't ready for this approach. Usually they say they do not want to create more complaints or suggest that there is a shortfall in service. They feel threatened by the possibility of criticism. In short we believe they are misguided. Quality begins with you; only you can improve what you do and only if you know how good it is. Finding out is not the challenge; the challenge lies in dealing with the knowledge.

Managing complaints

Complaints are a quality indicator which informs organisations how well they are delivering their services. In this respect complaints are to be welcomed as feedback that managers can act on, even though the management of individual complaints may be challenging. Organisations which are highly customer-focused often refer to complaints as 'jewels'.

Under the wing of the Citizen's Charter a complaints task force was set up in June 1993 to review public service complaints systems. They identified a checklist by which to review all complaints systems. Complaints systems should:

- be easily accessible and well publicised
- be simple to understand and use
- allow speedy handling, with established time limits for action, and keep people informed of progress
- ensure a full and fair investigation

- respect people's desire for confidentiality
- address all the points at issue, provide an effective response and appropriate redress
- provide information to management so that services can be improved.

If you are a small voluntary organisation then you may find you can implement these principles in quite an informal way. Whether small or large, you will have to prepare volunteers for the eventuality that they may be complained about and that they could be helpful in responding to a complaint.

The first principles about access and simplicity clearly mean that you should have a well publicised route which complainants can follow and that the steps to making a complaint should be very simple. People should be able to find out easily how to complain and who to complain to. Speedy handling means that complainants should receive an answer promptly to the issue they have complained about. Larger organisations may divide their complaints into informal and formal types – informal being those that can usually be resolved on the spot and formal being those which may require an investigation and a written response. For the latter it may help to set standards about how long it should take you to acknowledge the complaint and to deliver a final response. These time standards should allow for a full investigation and, therefore, time to interview all the people concerned. Should this process involve volunteers more time should be allowed to take account of their more limited availability. The people involved will need to understand the importance of confidentiality in your complaints investigation, and you may have to reiterate this to volunteers.

The next principle requires you to ensure that you have covered every aspect of the complaint and have responded to these. Your response should state what action you are going to take and any points which you feel you cannot put right. You should consider what is appropriate in terms of redress, although there may be little you can do other than offer a full apology and a reassurance that you will try to ensure no future recurrence.

Finally, good complaints systems are only good if the organisation learns to improve the service that generates complaints. If you receive several complaints – say, one a week – then you need some simple method of analysing the themes that emerge from these so that you can take appropriate action. Often you will find that complainants are more upset by people's attitudes or the poor information they have been given rather than a breakdown in actual services. Should complaints involve the actions of volunteers then, at various points in this book, we have discussed useful approaches to selection, communication skills, getting your purpose across, and showing appreciation.

The mechanics of handling complaints is relatively straightforward, but there can be sensitivities with staff, particularly volunteers, who may be the subject of a complaint. As a manager, you should be alert to these, should ensure that your investigation is detailed enough to understand the volunteer's role in any complaint, and should give any volunteers upset about allegations involving them the opportunity to talk through their feelings.

There are also useful ways in which you can involve volunteers in managing complaints, such as researching service provision or legislation. You may be lucky enough to find a volunteer who has experience in complaints management from their work setting. Using complaints in an anonymised way, as a case approach to training volunteers, is a helpful way of discussing their involvement, helping to clarify values and identifying further needs.

Advocacy

We mention advocacy here because it is a definite client-centred activity targeted at improving services. In times of rapid change the mobile, literate and articulate are able to argue their case for the services they need or demonstrate their eligibility. Much recent legislation – for example, the NHS and Community Care Act 1990, the Disabled Persons Act 1986, the Mental Health Act 1983, and also various charter standards – claim to improve services or protect people's rights. Despite all this there are many elderly, disabled or disadvantaged people who are unaware even that their rights are being infringed or that a particular law or charter exists to address their situation.

Of course we all recognise the work of the Citizens' Advice Bureau which can be found in many high streets around the country. But, again, people have to be able to get into the town and also have the confidence to discuss their problems with a stranger. By the nature of their difficulties many of these people will be in touch with voluntary organisations and you, or volunteers working with you, may be acting as their advocates.

We shall clarify here what we mean by advocacy and types of advocacy. The principles of acting as an advocate involve acting responsibly for, or 'pleading the cause for', another person who is unable to speak or act for themselves. It requires that you ascertain precisely the wishes of the client and be able to confidently express them. To be effective as an advocate you need to motivate other people to see things from the viewpoint of the client you are representing. You need to identify those most appropriate to put the case to, those who can effect change for your client. For this reason you need a sound knowledge of the rules, procedures and protocols of the organisation to whom you are advocating. You need sound communication skills, especially an ability to challenge others yet at the same time handle and resolve conflict. You will, of course, recognise these qualities as essential to the effective manager.

arena

Arena is the newest imprint in the Ashgate Publishing Group. It gathers together titles on social work and policy, education and health and aims to help professionals put theory into practice.

Please fill in the section below and return this Freepost reply card to us so that we can send you details of forthcoming publications in the areas that interest you.

Name _____

Job title and Institution (if relevant) _____

Address _____

_____ Postcode _____

_____

Please send me information on the books you publish in the following subject areas:

☐ Health ☐ Popular Culture/Youth Studies ☐ Education ☐ Advisory Services

☐ Social Reference ☐ Professional Social Work ☐ Police/Criminology Studies

If you know anyone else who would appreciate this service please give their details here:

_____

_____

☐ *Please tick this box if you do not wish to receive information from other organizations*

2K051

Arena
Marketing Services Manager
Gower House
Croft Road
Aldershot
Hampshire
GU11 3BR

One of the problems of being an advocate is knowing when to advocate. Clearly there are more obvious times – for example, when a person is confused or lacks the necessary communication skills to obtain their rights. Knowing when not to advocate is also very important. Can you imagine your feelings if someone were to start making decisions for you, which affected your life and which you thought you could handle yourself? We should remember that we do not always make the right decisions for ourselves. Part of being human is being allowed to make mistakes and learn from them. It can be very tempting as a volunteer, or indeed as a paid professional, to make decisions for clients because we feel that they are not making the correct choice. Wherever possible we should be sure, by confirming with clients, that they want us to act for them and clarify the outcome they are seeking.

Volunteers are often thought to be well suited to being advocates as they are distanced from the conflicts faced by both family members and professionals. Many examples of schemes involving volunteers exist nationwide. Well known schemes are operated by MIND for people with mental health problems and services operated by Age Concern for older people. Many health and social services departments also recruit and train volunteers for work with their own clients. Whilst these schemes share a similar philosophy they may differ in their mode of operation and may vary from client to client, service to service and adapt to meet the needs of local geographical areas. Papers produced in 1985 by the Kings Fund Centre 'Mental Health and Welfare Rights' and in 1993 by NAHAT 'Investing in Patients Representatives' together with a series of publications from GPMH (Good Practices in Mental Health) identify a range of these.

Types of advocacy

Four principal types of advocacy exist:

1 **Client self-advocacy.** Here the client is encouraged or empowered to speak up for himself. This would be the ultimate goal of all advocacy groups.
2 **Legal advocacy.** Legal advocacy empowers the client via access to more formal redress – for instance, by lawyers or welfare rights advisers. It still requires adherence to the fundamental principles referred to above.
3 **Collective or class advocacy.** This type refers to relatively large organisations which pursue the interests of a category of people. Such organisations may use paid officers and volunteers.
4 **Citizen advocacy.** Here the client is empowered by the support of another independent person to represent them. The advocate represents the interests of the client as if they were his own. This may be the first step towards achieving self-advocacy.

You as a manager, and your volunteers will most probably be in one of the last two categories. Ways in which you might undertake advocacy might include:

- **Informal advocacy:** This involves giving options to the person you are helping and supporting them once they have made their decision. You may assist or negotiate on behalf of the person you are helping when dealing with people in authority.
- **Formal advocacy:** This entails taking up specific issues or challenging the administrative procedures set up by authorities. You will need to have a good understanding of the organisation's relevant procedures.
- **Public advocacy:** Here you would act for wider change, either directly in the way that you represent your organisation, client or purpose or indirectly, by the model you present to others as you go about your day-to-day activities.

Undertaking public advocacy means bringing areas of concern formally into the public eye with a view to bringing about the development or change to policy and procedures and changing attitudes.

Supporting volunteer advocates

Much has been written about whether those directly giving services (whether paid or unpaid) can be advocates. Most people take the view that the advocate should be independent of service provision because of their potential conflicts of interest – trying to do right both by the organisation and by the person. This may lend further support to advocacy being a role for volunteers. However, being an advocate can create certain conflicts and therefore the need for support from managers. One fairly common source of conflict is in trying to advocate for informal carers and those they are caring for when each expresses different wishes. Each is entitled to representation, and seeking compromise may be the best solution to aim for.

The training of advocates will involve the acquisition of a range of skills and knowledge, including communication skills and knowledge of appropriate legislation and procedures. Such training should be ongoing in order to develop the individual, it should afford support in the role, and should seek to convince the volunteer that it is all right to ask for support.

We have talked about the need to respect confidentiality previously and we need to reiterate it here. Advocates may need support when they are holding difficult or stressful information in confidence. This may involve talking through issues in an anonymous way. Advocates may occasionally need a way out of a situation which you, as a manager, have to create for them, often by being willing to take their place.

It is possible that some volunteers may undertake advocacy within staffed accommodation. Research has shown that staff may see the introduction of independent advocates as a challenge to their own beliefs that they are adequately representing their clients. As such staff will have feelings of being devalued as a result. This will be another situation to which you should be sensitive.

Advocacy schemes can give staff and service users the opportunity to forge new partnerships, enable them to meet with those people for whom they care on more equal terms, and also leads to better joint decision-making. It will be important both to communicate to volunteers the philosophy and principle of the service as well as to identify working protocols for its implementation.

9 Putting it all together

We set out to write this book because we felt strongly that there was a timely need for it. If anything, the experience of researching and writing it has reinforced our view that it is very much needed. That is not to say that we don't know some impressive managers in voluntary organisations, but we have met many who are anxious about the changing times ahead and how they will cope. We have also met many volunteers who hope for better management.

We took the stance at the beginning that many managers in the voluntary sector would find it useful to review a broad range of core management principles. This we have tried to do fairly concisely and creatively. We took a particular view that, because of the large volunteer contribution to the work of many voluntary organisations, managers needed to manage them effectively. In fact, for many managers, being an effective manager in the voluntary sector must be synonymous with working effectively with volunteers. Thus, we have tried to explore the implications of better management from the particular and practical perspective of working with volunteers. This has led us to develop some specific management issues and emphasise managerial skills and qualities appropriate to these situations.

Cycles of activity

Having got to this point, the 'putting it all together' stage, it would be good if we could offer a simple formula to convert everyone into 'all-singing, all-dancing' managers. Well, there's no chance of that! However, there are still some good and helpful ideas that we can review here. It is useful to view good management as a cycle of activity: begin by defining your aims and objectives, work up a plan, choose and develop the people to deliver it, monitor progress and, finally, match the results with your intended goal.

Of course, this sounds far too simple, and indeed it is! If you recall Mintzberg's theories introduced in Chapter 1 you will realise that the day-to-day practice of management is a much more chaotic and piecemeal affair. Nevertheless, we can develop the cycle view by explaining management in practice as being immersed in many cycles of activity at the same time. Each cycle may be at a different stage, of different planned length and possibly involve different people. Some cycles become very extended, some foreshortened, some are repeated many times and some are stillborn. This begins to approach the complexity that Mintzberg speaks of. Day to day there is an art in purposeful prioritising of each cycle of activity and what you want to achieve next.

Present and future planning

You may also remember the 'helicopter ride' we took in Chapter 1. Here we were talking about the importance of seeing the wood from the trees by being able to take an objective overview of everything going on. Here we also mentioned the importance of being able to cope with the present and plan for the future at the same time. Future planning requires us to continually enhance our visioning skills. Using the cyclical approach we must regularly ask ourselves 'learning' type questions, such as:

- How is what we are doing today contributing to our wider objectives?
- What is everyone else doing that will help or hinder what I'm doing?
- How well did the job we've just finished work out? How could we improve on it?
- How well are we fulfilling our role in the community? How do we actually know this?
- From what we've just done what have we learned about gaps in services? Can we do anything about these?

These types of questions should help us to avoid the 'We've always done it this way' trap. In Chapter 3 we discussed the historical and cultural reasons for the unquestioning maintenance of the status quo. Good managers will recognise that there is almost nothing we do which, after consideration, we cannot improve on. Using volunteers to help make this learning contribution together is an important part of managing them effectively. In Chapter 5 we covered the importance of job design, particularly the wholeness of jobs, as a way of motivating volunteers, and as an aid to keeping them in Chapter 7.

Look to yourself

At the outset we emphasised that becoming a better manager was an investment in yourself. We reiterate that here. You should congratulate yourself on reading this far. Some of you may be fortunate enough to work for organisations that invest in staff development. All too often this is not the case, although there is often good intention with poor implementation. Organisations tend to expect you to deliver the goods regardless of whether or not they have made the investment in you. But good management skills not only help you get what you need in your current role but are transferable to other roles both within and beyond your current organisation.

Your organisation has many responsibilities towards you. But you, as a manager, need to accept a great deal of responsibility for yourself. These responsibilities include such things as: being alert to your changing situation; clarifying your role in your organisation; analysing your strengths, weaknesses, boundaries and so on; managing your own stress (within limits); motivating and supporting your staff; and treating your staff fairly. You can look to your organisation for help with much of this, but once you accept these personal responsibilities it is easier to accept also the need to invest your time in making them more manageable. Volunteers will look to you as a representative of the organisation for support. You will serve them well by sharpening their self-management skills too. Your success may be a credit to both, but your failure is more likely to be seen as personal.

'Walk the talk'

By now we've all learnt to walk. In management, 'walking' is used to describe various interesting activities. 'Walking the talk' very simply describes being genuine or, more accurately, being seen to be genuine and committed, or practising what you preach. Similarly you may have heard of 'management by walking about' – this implies that you should get out and about to see what is actually going on in your organisation rather than relying on reports and second-hand information.

Several aspects of what we might call 'walking' behaviour are important. First, do you think you can find out everything that is going on from sitting in your office? And if so, how accurate do you think the picture will be? Often information is 'massaged' to look more positive for those people who don't come to find out for themselves. Progress reports can sound a little more optimistic than the situation on the ground. Second, and more importantly, 'walking the job' is an opportunity to convey your interest in, and commitment to, both the volunteers and the job they are doing. Do you remember the Blake and Mouton grid in Chapter 4? This is a way of balancing task and team requirements. Remember also our player-manager in Chapter 1. Walking the job is not supposed to be an opportunity to slip back into whatever you used to do. Third, it is an opportunity to obtain feedback on your volunteers' needs. You can see how well they are coping, what their immediate concerns are and what support they need by going out to meet them. You can also get feedback about the quality of your good internal communications – are they doing exactly what you expected them to be doing? If the activity is in a public setting you can also get some impression about the quality of services being given at the point of delivery. Finally, it provides you with the opportunity to give direct feedback to volunteers about how well they are doing. Praise is usually highly valued, especially if given by someone they respect. The same usually applies to advice on how they might do something better.

We apologise if the above sounds obvious by now. It may be that the way you work means you are in constant touch with volunteers anyway. The most important point here is to convey to volunteers that you not only value what they are doing but that, by showing an interest, you value them personally.

Wide-awake management

Learning to juggle is fairly easy. With reasonable coordination you can keep three balls up in the air after a few hours' practice. Management is considerably harder; you have to keep all the balls up in the air all the time. Earlier we described management very simply as getting the right job done well. Since then we've added some complexity to that definition. The key qualities of efficiency and effectiveness are always worth applying as an acid test to everything you are doing.

But being wide-awake to management is not simply about keeping all the balls in the air at the same time. We know we can't do everything: we have to sort the 'now' from 'later' balls, to know which ones we must keep up at all costs and which one we could safely drop. We have to be able to make room for more, sometimes unexpectedly. If we develop our volunteers well we are being wide-awake to creating this extra capacity.

Much of what we have described earlier in the book is skill-based. You can learn to be better at managing time and money, improving communication, delegation and so on. You can even learn to do many of these things at the same time. The special quality of being wide-awake to everything, of being proactive, thinking ahead, thinking through implications, working out what impact you're having, and being several steps in front of others takes more time. But it can come if you work at it. It's not a case of 'Miracles we do at once, the impossible takes a little longer'. It's a case of making conscious efforts to develop your managerial awareness, to continually check your own progress, to reflect on what you and your team are achieving. You can ask yourself simple and frequent questions to check yourself: 'How am I doing?', 'How are we doing?', 'Could I do this better next time?', 'What am I missing?' In voluntary organisations the effectiveness of the interactions you have with volunteers can be a useful yardstick. They are a valuable source of feedback as to how well you, the wider department and the organisation is doing. But you have to *ask* occasionally. You might even start waking up other people too.

Conclusion

We hope you can appreciate that there is no simple formula to effective management in voluntary organisations. We can't reduce it all to three things you should do when you get out of bed every morning! But, if we had to have a go, it would be something like:

1   *Remember that change is a constant.* Things may have changed since yesterday. Try to prioritise how best you spend your time every day, but keep an eye on the bigger picture and any new directions indicated.
2   *Try to find a few minutes every day to reflect on what you're doing and what you've just finished.* Could you have done anything more effectively or more efficiently, particularly in the way you involved volunteers? Invest in them; invest in yourself.
3   *Try to show volunteers you value them,* by thoughtful consideration of the jobs you give them, by asking their opinions, by respecting their views, by honesty, by trying to work alongside them occasionally, by giving them feedback about their performance.

Lastly, try and find some time for yourself!
    Good luck.

Appendix 1:   Writing your CV

You need some advantages in the jobs market when there are too few jobs for too many applicants. One of the best ways of taking advantage is to submit an impressive CV. A CV is not just a document which collects together your life's experiences to show your next potential employer. You have to employ some marketing skills in writing it if you want it to take you from a mere applicant (one of many) to a person on a shortlist (one of few).

Your CV must make an instant impression as those involved in selection may have very little else to go on. It should impress both by its presentation and its content. We shall look at each of these in turn.

Presentation

Your CV must look like a professional quality document but not be too ostentatious. It will create an impression about you regardless of whoever has produced it for you, so you must consider what impression you want its appearance to convey. Below are some simple guidelines to follow to give your CV a favourable appearance.

Do:

- *Have it typed/word-processed in an easily readable print style.* Serif print styles are more readable than sans serif. Employers like to see your handwriting, which you can provide in a letter, but a laser printed CV gives a much better impression. If typing, then ensure you use a decent ribbon as your CV may have to be photocopied. Better still, send two copies.
- *Use a clear format with bold headings for each section* (see 'Contents' below).

- *Check the spelling and grammar thoroughly.* The CV is a test of how well and how accurately you can express yourself, and of your care over detail. If in doubt ask someone to proofread it.
- *Sign it at the end.* It adds a nice personal touch.
- *Assemble all the pages, numbered, in the right order and staple them together.* Include good quality photocopies of any certificates you are sending, not the originals.

Don't:

- *Put it in a plastic wallet* which requires anyone to take it out to read it. It's tempting for recruiters not to bother when they've got too many.
- *Make it too long!* Recruiters at this stage are unlikely to be interested in your memoirs. Again research shows that 3–4 pages is the maximum length you should write. Write concisely and without jargon. If you can reduce it to one or two pages so much the better. If you have a couple of pages of publications then submit an appendix. Think about dispensing with a cover sheet.

Contents

Before you start to write your CV, find out as much about the job as you can. What clues are there in the advertisement to who is needed. What does the job description and the person specification sent with the information package indicate? What are the clear strengths, skills and qualities expected for the job which must be emphasised in your CV? Whatever you think the critical skills and qualities the recruiter requires for the job you should try to address these on the first visible page of your CV.

Format

The most commonly used format is a chronological one which details your experience in date order. It should contain eight sections.

1   *Personal details*

Name
Address
Telephone No. (day and evening)
Age/date of birth
Marital status (optional)

2   *Education*

Include brief details of schooling and examinations passed. Then identify professional training and qualifications gained and those you are studying for. List in date order. Include full-time, day release, evening, correspondence courses.

3   *Personal skills and attributes*

This is a really important section of your CV which you must ensure is on the front page. Recruiters will be looking for the skills and attributes you have that separate you from the others. Tell them what you think you are good at doing. Training and qualifications alone are no guarantee of skills. Have a look at the skills register at the end of this Appendix to see if there are any ideas here that you could use.

4   *Summary of current job and responsibilities*

This too is an important section to try to get on the front page. As already said, most recruiters, whilst looking for something particular to the job, will also be looking for evidence of achievements and enthusiasm. Don't just say what you do but put down what you've achieved successfully. Try to make duties sound like your good ideas. Indicate something of the management style you use, how you get on with people, how well you work in teams, how you bring about change and so on. Try to give some evidence of breadth, the size of your team, the range of people you liaise with, the different projects you are involved in and so on.

5   *Previous employment*

List in chronological order the jobs you've had from first to last. Identify the position and the company. Briefly describe the responsibilities you had in those jobs held in the last five years. Try to show some career progression. If this is early in your career you should mention relevant voluntary activities, holiday jobs, training activities, work experience and so forth. If you have a long career history of change you will have to be concise, especially about the early years!

6   *Activities and interests*

Recruiters generally like to see some evidence of your personality from the 'roundedness' of your activities and interests. You may need to play along a little! Don't put down so much that the recruiter is left wondering when you'd fit the job in.

7   Other information

Much of this will be optional, depending on the job in question. The common things to consider are:

- possession of a (clean) driving licence
- membership of professional/technical associations
- computer literacy.

There will be jobs where it will also be relevant to include any of the following:

- papers/books published
- papers given at conferences
- work experience abroad
- languages spoken
- passport
- special awards you have received
- health status.

8   References

Identify two people who can be contacted for a recent reference about you. Give name, address, job title, place of work and telephone no. References can be taken up by telephone or letter. Be prepared to use a range of people, depending on the job you are applying for. Don't be afraid to ask referees what they are going to say about you. You may be surprised! Pick referees who think you are reliable, enthusiastic, willing to learn and can work in a team.

Finally . . .

1   Check all the documents you are sending back with your job application to make sure you haven't missed any – for example:

- Application form
- CV
- Evidence of qualifications
- Photograph
- Evidence of driving licence
- Covering letter.

Make sure you have included the right number of copies and they are all secured together.

2   Keep a copy of your CV and anything else you have sent. Make sure you know what you've said off by heart and be prepared to answer questions about any of it.

3   Send your application in early before the cut-off date. This can create an impression of enthusiasm. For the same reason send it by first-class mail. If you have any doubt, or you are sending personal documents, you should use recorded delivery.

4   Good luck!

Skills register

You may find this list of skill words useful in constructing your CV.

Advertised	Helped	Planned
Administered	Hired	Prepared
Analysed	Implemented	Presented
Arranged	Improved	Promoted
Assessed	Initiated	Project-managed
Assembled	Inspected	Published
Budgeted	Interviewed	Recruited
Built	Invented	Repaired
Cared for	Investigated	Researched
Classified	Judged	Scheduled
Contributed to	Kept the books	Secured
Controlled	Listened	Set up
Coordinated	Liaised	Sold
Created	Made	Solved
Debated	Marketed	Sorted
Demonstrated	Managed	Supervised
Designed	Motivated	Taught
Discovered	Negotiated	Tested
Edited	Operated	Trained
Evaluated	Organised	Verified
Forecast	Performed	Won
Grew	Persuaded	Written
Guided	Pioneered	
Handled	Piloted	

Appendix 2: Writing a reference

There will be many occasions as a manager when you will be asked to give a reference, either for someone currently working for you or who has done so in the past. This may be for a volunteer who is now seeking paid employment.

Usually the request will be for a reference in writing, but it is becoming more common to be asked to supply a reference on the telephone. Requests for written references do vary in the information and detail that potential employers want. Some will give you a structured format for the reply. In the absence of this, the standard information you should give includes:

- how long you have known the candidate and in what context – for example, as a personal friend, work colleague, manager and so on
- the skills and qualities you think the candidate has in respect of the job being applied for
- other general comments on skills, performance, or significant achievements that you think may be relevant
- areas of concern you might have about the candidate, if any
- candidate's sickness and absence record.

An example of a reference is provided below. This is likely to be the sort of information you would give in a telephone reference as well as in writing.

Example: Job reference

Radical Vague Charity
Flat Hill
Beckenham
BE2 4LL
10.4.95

Dear Sir,

Thank you for the opportunity to provide Ronald Biggs with a reference. I'm pleased to hear he wants to put his fundraising skills to good use.

I have known Ronald for nine months as he has been with us as a volunteer since last summer. He has been very helpful to us in suggesting fundraising ideas and coordinated a big pre-Christmas initiative which raised over £3000. His communication skills are clear and his planning is meticulous. He gets on well with others, has a good sense of humour and has been helpful in supporting other volunteers in the team. He is very good at motivating those less interested.

From the job description you sent me I feel sure he will be able to act on his own initiative and has a creative side, often helping us with posters and leaflets. I am not sure why he left his previous employment as he has always been a little vague on that, but may be more open with you.

I cannot comment on his sickness record directly but in the nine months he was with us he has always been reliable and timely in turning up.

I hope you find this useful.

Yours sincerely,

Phil McSweeney
Area Manager

The point of the reference is to give the prospective employer some additional and hopefully objective information on which to base a decision. If you have been sent the job description for the job applied for then use this as a guide for the specific qualities and skills you should comment on. The reference may not be consulted until after the interview. The reason employers also ask for two or three references is also to ensure they get a balanced picture, and preferably one of reasonable consensus.

You should seek to be accurate and fair in your comments, commenting both on strengths and weaknesses. If you find it difficult to be explicit about weaknesses you should suggest that the potential employer explores a particular issue further with the candidate to satisfy themselves. On strengths, again, you must be fair. There have been some legal cases where an employer has sought to sue a previous employer for stating an employee had skills that they clearly hadn't. The way to manage a poor performer is not by giving them a glowing reference in the hope you can get rid of them.

We would also remind you here about equal opportunity issues, as mentioned in Chapter 5. Obviously you should not state anything discriminatory in a reference, such as imputing that poor performance is due to single parenthood, disability and so on.

It is a good idea to keep copies of references given, especially as people who use you as a referee are likely to do so again. Candidates may quite legitimately ask you what you would say in a reference. As a good manager it should cause you no problems to give a copy of a reference to the candidate. You ought not to find yourself saying something in a reference that you haven't previously discussed with the candidate.

Appendix 3: Writing a short report

It is increasingly likely that, as a manager or even as a volunteer, you will at some time be asked to write or contribute to a report. This may be to another organisation, to your Board of Trustees, or to a management or project team. The report could be about any number of issues: a service you have provided to a user; a project you have managed; an incident that has occurred; a report in support of a bid for resources and so on.

However, all good reports have certain properties in common:

1 **A clear structure.** Key sections should include:

   - a title page showing the title, who report is to and from, the date of the report
   - a summary
   - an introduction
   - the main body of the report - the main account of the problem or issue
   - conclusions
   - recommendations
   - any references or further reading required
   - any appendices.

2 **Clarity and brevity of communication.** To have any benefit most reports need to be widely read and understood. You can influence this by the way you write and present it. It needs to be concise but also to reflect substantiated evidence or arguments for and against the recommendations you make. Keep to the facts and try to avoid the use of unnecessary jargon. The front page is particularly important because it is likely to determine whether the rest of it gets read. The title and who it is for should be clear and the summary should be no longer than a couple of short paragraphs.

Don't worry if a report appears short. If you have said all you need to say then there is no need to embellish it.

It is the convention to write in the third person and the present tense, although exceptions would be where you are making a statement in a legal context or describing action you have taken. If you are mentioning people by name in your report then let them read it before publication, unless legal reasons prevent this. It may save you some embarrassment later.

If the report is in respect of an incident from which legal proceedings may arise you would be wise to consult with a more senior manager, your organisation's legal adviser and, if an internal matter, your own union or professional representative.

Appendix 4: Giving a presentation

As a manager you are most likely to be asked at some time to give a presentation. Examples of topics for presentations may include:

- giving a talk to another organisation on the work of your service
- speaking to a group of people interested in joining your group
- introducing a project to members of you own organisation with a view to gaining their support
- giving a report to your management team concerning your progress
- training sessions in which you are giving people new ideas or encouraging them to reflect on their present practice.

From the above list you can see that the range and types of presentation can be quite varied. Some you may find enjoyable and some may be more demanding than others. For instance, we probably all like to share our favourite topics with others; here we feel safe and can convey a sense of enthusiasm to our audience. On the other hand, the presentation of a major change initiative to a group of sceptical colleagues may be very daunting.

As experienced teachers we would reassure you that feeling nervous or apprehensive is not at all unusual. Indeed it may be a stimulus to making a good presentation. The person who feels overconfident may not be sensitive to the audience and may not be aware of how the message is being received. A degree of 'stage nerves' is normal and helps keep us on our toes.

Preparing the presentation

There are two key secrets to any good presentation: knowledge of your subject and sound preparation. When you are first considering giving your presentation, identify the following:

- Who will you be speaking to?
- How many people will be present?
- What type of venue will you be performing in?
- How long have you got to speak?
- Will your presentation have to follow on from, or fit in with, another?
- Will you require any special apparatus or materials?

This information, and the time spent in preparing your presentation, will be most helpful to your success.

Who will you be speaking to?

The composition of your audience, their present knowledge of the subject on which you intend speaking and even their cultural and social background can influence the approach which you take and the language that you may use. Can you safely use jargon or does it need to be in absolutely plain English? The likely response of the audience to your presentation, whether favourable or apprehensive, will be of help in shaping your talk to address individual needs.

How many people will be present?

A formal lecture seems inappropriate when speaking to a small group, but it is a very practical approach for a large group where social contact is limited. Sometimes the size of group is critical to the outcome of the exercise. For example, if you want to involve the group in sharing experiences or develop interpersonal skills then you will wish to limit the size, perhaps to 10 or 12 maximum.

Consider the estimated number of people present and adjust your presentation style to them. It's also useful to know if you will be giving handouts.

The type of venue

Will this be a large auditorium, a village hall or a small room? In the same way as we discussed the numbers of people, the environment will effect the way in which you address the audience. Be aware of possible interruptions caused by passers-by. In one venue we were given the room used as the route between other classrooms and the coffee room – and no one synchronised the coffee breaks! Find out also about the availability of seating and tables and whether they can be moved. Do you want to present to rows of people, in conference style, or small groups? It is also wise to make sure that the venue can accommodate your teaching aids. It is most embarrassing to discover that the room doesn't have a power point.

Research and preparation

The secret of any presentation lies in thoroughly researching and understanding the topic which you are addressing. Think of the likely consequences of your input and consider the likely questions which your audience may ask.

If you are new to giving presentations you may benefit from rehearsing your talk to a friend or into a tape recorder. If neither of these appeal to you, do spend time reading through your 'script'. This is the best way to get your timing right too.

To assist your presentation it can be useful to make up small cards with your key words or phrases listed in order of presentation. These are not as obvious and offputting to your audience as a wad of papers. In our experience the latter can get out of order at the most inconvenient time!

The presentation itself

To keep the presentation lively think of how you respond as a listener to the presentations of others. What retains your interest and what detracts from the subject matter? The use of a light joke or an appropriate cartoon often helps. Remember also to vary your tone appropriately and not give a flat monologue. Don't be afraid of showing your enthusiasm for your subject or introducing a sense of humour into the proceedings. It is also a good idea to read and be sensitive to your audience – for example, to expand where interest is shown – but remember to keep to time.

Finally, ask the audience questions to increase participation and praise people's contributions. We can, after all, learn from one another and two-way participation is encouraging to us all.

When your presentation is complete try to seek some feedback, either formally through a short checklist or in discussion with the person who invited you to speak. Alternatively, obtain some informal feedback from your audience over refreshments. If you listen to the balanced observations and comments of others you will begin to develop both confidence and your own style of presentation.

Glossary

agency
: Any organisation, statutory or private, which provides social care, health care or housing services in the community.

assertiveness
: Being able to state clearly your needs and beliefs without diminishing yourself or anyone else.

assessment
: The process of objectively defining needs and determining eligibility for assistance against stated policy criteria. It is a participative process involving the applicant, their carers and other relevant agencies.

care package
: A combination of services designed to meet the assessed needs of a person requiring care in the community.

care planning
: The process of negotiation between assessor, applicant, carers and other relevant agencies on the most appropriate ways of meeting assessed needs within available resources and incorporating them into an individual care plan.

carer
: A person who is not employed to provide the care in question by any body in the exercise of its function under enactment. Normally, this will be a person who is looking after another adult in the home who is frail, ill and/or mentally or physically disabled, and where the dependency relationship 'exceeds that implicit in normally dependent relationships' between family members.

care management	Any strategy for managing and coordinating and reviewing service for the individual client in a way that provides for continuity of care and accountability to both the client and the managing agency.
care manager	Any practitioner who undertakes all, or most, of the 'tasks' of care management, who may carry a budgetary responsibility but is not involved in any direct service provision.
case management	This is now substituted in many localities by the term 'care management' or used to mean the same as 'key worker'.
collaboration	A partnership of joint working between all authorities and agencies involved in planning and delivering community services.
commissioning	The function of specifying what services are required, and then conferring upon an agency the duty to provide these services, usually by mutually agreed contract.
community care	The provision of services and support which people who are affected by problems of ageing, mental illness, mental handicap or physical or sensory disability need to be able to live as independently as possible in their own homes, or in 'homely' settings in the community.
CCP	Community Care Plan.
community care services	Services which a local authority may provide or arrange to be provided under any of the following provisions: 1 Part III of the National Assistance Act 1948 2 Section 45 of the Health Services and Public Health Act 1968 3 Section 21 of, and Schedule 8 to, the National Health Service Act 1977 and 4 Section 117 of the Mental Health Act 1983.
consultation	A dialogue between local authorities, commissioners and providers of care, service users and their carers to ensure a shared appreciation of local needs and to agree a local framework for meeting these needs.

consumer	The end user, client, patient or carer.
contract	Any agreement enforceable by law.
culture	A common identity based on a number of factors such as memories, ethnic identity, child-rearing, class, income, religious upbringing, division of family roles – cultures continually evolve both for individuals and communities. Organisations are also said to have cultures – the set of beliefs and values which pervade it and which determine how things are done.
day care	Communal care normally provided in a setting away from the user's place of residence, with paid or voluntary carers present. Day care can cover a very wide range of services.
demography	The study of statistics of births, deaths and diseases to illustrate conditions and changes in the community.
DHA	District Health Authority. The DHA is responsible, within the resources available, for identifying the health-care needs of its resident population and for securing through its contracts with providers, a package of services to reflect those needs. The DHA has a responsibility – with the LA and FHSA – to ensure satisfactory collaboration and joint planning with other agencies. It is accountable to the regional health authority for the satisfactory discharge of its responsibilities. From 1 April 1996, DHAs and FHSAs effectively combine as one commissioning organisation.
DHSS	Department of Health and Social Security.
Director of Social Services	The non-elected officer appointed by a local social services authority to be responsible to them for the operation of their social services functions.
disabled	Having a physical, emotional or learning impediment that requires the provision of specific facilities to enable the individual to fully participate in, contribute to and benefit from their personal life and the full rights and responsibilities and citizenship.

discharge plan   Plan drawn up before a patient's discharge from hospital making appropriate arrangements for any necessary continuing care or treatment. The plans should include a checklist of action to be taken by all those concerned with the patient.

domiciliary care   Care arrangements/services which support an individual living in a private household either alone or in the care of a relative or other carer.

ethnicity   A group sharing some or all of the following traits, customs, lifestyle, religion, language or nationality.

enabling authority   An authority whose main function is to secure and fund services to reflect the assessed needs of its local population; selecting the most cost-effective from among its own provision and that of other agencies.

equal opportunities   Policies which recognise inequality in respect of race, gender, sexual orientation, colour, religion or disability and which seek to ensure fairness and equality in operation – for example, recruitment, personal development, advancement and so on.

FHSA   Family Health Services Authority. FHSAs are responsible for managing the services provided under the NHS by family doctors, dentists, community pharmacists and ophthalmic opticians. FHSAs are accountable to RHAs and work in close collaboration with DHAs. (See DHA.)

HA   Health Authorities. For the purposes of this book, this includes Regional Health Authorities, District Health Authorities, Family Health Services Authorities and, where appropriate, Special Health Authorities and Special Health Services Authorities. (See DHA.)

health care   Medical care which is provided by the National Health Service. It is recognised that there is no clear divide between health care and social care; this interface is for local discussion and agreement between health and local authorities.

housing association	Section I of the Housing Associations Act 1985 defines a housing association as a society, body of trustees or company which does not trade for profit, and whose purpose or objective is to provide, construct, improve or manage housing accommodation.
inspection units	The group of staff responsible for the inception of residential care homes and, at the discretion of the local authority, other quality control functions.
inspection sector	Individuals, bodies or organisations not wholly maintained or controlled by a government department or any other authority or body instituted by a Special Act of Parliament or incorporated by Royal Charter.
JCC	Joint Consultative Committee.
joint plans	CCPs which are jointly produced by health authorities and local authorities; although this is not mandatory, all CCPs should be at least complementary.
key worker	The service-providing practitioner who has most contact with the user and who may undertake a similar coordinating function to a care manager but remains involved in direct service provision.
local authority (LA)	The council of a county, a metropolitan district, a London borough or the Common Council of the City of London.
local housing authority	A local authority responsible for the provision of housing and related services. A local housing authority is defined in sections 1, 2 and 4 of the Housing Act 1985 as a district council, a London borough council, the Common Council of the City of London or the Council of the Isles of Scilly.
mixed economy	The use of independent providers (including the voluntary sector) alongside good quality public services, to increase the available range of options.
NAHAT	National Association of Health Authorities and Trusts.

NCVO   National Council for Voluntary Organisations.

NHS   National Health Service.

NHSE   The NHS Executive: the Department of Health's managing group for the National Health Service.

not-for-profit sector   The voluntary/charitable sector in which no profits are made on services provided.

nursing home care   Care provided in a registered nursing home as defined in Part III, section 21 of the Registered Homes Act 1984; this entails a state registered nurse being on the premises at all times, and the provision of medical care by a general practitioner.

outcomes   The contribution to the wellbeing of the client of services provided.

outputs   The range, quantity and quality of services provided.

planning agreement An agreement between authorities involved in planning care services to establish the funding and commissioning of health and social services for those in need.

policy guidance   A statement from the Department of Health which elaborates on a legislative framework and sets out what authorities need to do. By virtue of section 7 (1) of the Local Authority Social Services Act 1970, local authorities are under a duty to act in accordance with general guidance issued by the Secretary of State in the exercise of their social services functions.

private sector   Non-voluntary agencies in the independent sector.

provider   Any person, group of persons, or organisations supplying a community care service.

public sector   Any facility maintained or controlled by a government department or local authority or any other authority or body instituted by special Act of Parliament or incorporated by Royal Charter.

purchaser	The budget holder who contracts to buy a service.
RHA	Regional Health Authority. These are the Centre's agents for managing change and for ensuring the implementation of government policies. They allocate resources to DHAs and FHSAs and monitor their performance in achieving agreed objectives. From 1 April 1996, RHAs became Regional Offices – part of the DoH. (See DHA.)
registration	In the case of residential care homes, the means by which statutory control is exercised by local authorities under the terms of the Registered Homes Act 1984. Certain homes, including those managed or provided by local authorities, are exempt from the requirements to register.
service specification	A set of minimum requirements relating to a service to be supplied.
sexism	The personal and institutional differentiation of power and status between the sexes which limit the opportunities for girls and women as employees and service users.
social care	Non-medical care which is arranged, and may be provided, by local authorities and for which authorities may assess client's ability to pay and charge accordingly. It is recognised that there is no clear divide between health care and social care; this interface is for local discussion and agreement between health authorities and local authorities.
Social Services Authority (SSA)	The council of a non-metropolitan county, metropolitan district, London borough, or the Common Council of the City of London.
Social Services Committee (SSC)	The committee of the social services authority in which its social services functions are referred or delegated.
social services department (SSD)	The department of the social services authority headed by the Director of Social Services.

statutory sector   Those bodies required by parliamentary statute to provide a service, principally local authorities and health authorities.

TEC   Training and Enterprise Council.

voluntary sector   Voluntary organisations in which any surpluses are re-invested into the work of the organisation and managed by unpaid management committees, trustees or directors.

volunteer   A person who gives of their time freely, without coercion and for no financial reward.

References and further reading

Introduction / General

Carrington, L. (1994), 'The benefits of talking shop', *Personnel Today*, 17 May, p. 15.
de la Noy, M. (1987), *Acting as Friends: The Story of the Samaritans*, London: Constable.
Knapp, M. (1990), *Time is Money: The Cost of Volunteering in Britain Today*, London: Volunteer Centre UK.
Lloyd, T. (1993), *The Charity Business*, London: John Murray Ltd.
Loney, M. and Bobbock, R. (1991), *The State of the Market – Politics and Welfare in Contemporary Britain*, London: Age Publications.
Young, K. (1991), *Meeting the Needs of Strangers*, London: Gresham College.

Chapter 1   Me: the manager

Handy, C. (1985), *Understanding Organisations*, Harmondsworth: Penguin.
Handy, C. (1988), *Understanding Voluntary Organisations*, Harmondsworth: Penguin.
Mintzberg, H. (1973), *The Nature of Managerial Work*, London: Harper & Row.
Pugh, D.S. and Hickson, D.J. (1989), *Writers on Organisations* (4th edn), Harmondsworth: Penguin.
Stewart, R. (1985), *The Reality of Management*, London: Pan Books.
Workplace Communications (1988), ACAS Advisory Booklet No. 8.

Chapter 2   All change

Barclay Report (1982), *Social Workers: Their Role and Tasks*, London: Bedford Square Press.

Bulmer, M. (1987), *The Social Basis of Community Care*, London: Allen & Unwin.

Carey, S. (1993), *Older People and Community Care*, London: OPCS.

Contracting In or Out (1989), London: NCVO.

Department of Health (DoH) (1989), *Caring for People: Community Care in the Next Decade and Beyond*, London: HMSO.

Department of Health (DoH) (1993), *Caring for People: Information Pack for the Voluntary and Private Sectors*, London: HMSO.

Department of Health and Social Security (DHSS) (1981), *Care in the Community: A Consultative Document on Moving Resources for Care in England*, London: HMSO.

Gutch, R. (1992), *Contracting Lessons from the US*, London: NCVO.

Heginbotham, C. (1990), *Return to Community (The Voluntary Ethic and Community Care)*, London: Bedford Square Press.

Jones, K., Brown, J. and Bradshaw, K. (1978), *Issues in Social Policy*, London: Routledge & Kegan Paul.

Lloyd, T. (1993), *The Charity Business*, London: John Murray Ltd.

Pater, J.E. (1981), *The Making of the National Health Service*, London: Kings Fund.

Pressland, T. (1990), *Volunteers and Community Care*, The Volunteer Centre.

Toffler, A. (1970), *Futureshock*, London: Bodley Head.

Tönnies, F. (1955), *Community and Association*, London: Routledge & Kegan Paul.

Walker, A. (1982), *Community Care: The Family, the State and Social Policy*, Oxford: Basil Blackwell/Martin Robertson.

Chapter 3:   Volunteers and the organisation

Handy, C. (1985), *Understanding Organisations*, Harmondsworth: Penguin.

Chapter 4:   Managing yourself effectively

Adair, J. (1987), *How to Manage Your Time*, New York: McGraw-Hill.

Back, K. (1982), *Assertiveness at Work*, New York: McGraw-Hill.

Blake, R. and Mouton. J. (1962), 'The Managerial Grid', *Advanced Management Office Executive*, **1** (9).

Clarke, S. (1992), *The Complete Fundraising Handbook*, The Directory of Social Change.

Dickinson, A. (1982), *A Woman in Your Own Right: Assertiveness and You*, London: Quartet Books.

Doherty, C. and Firkin, P. (1993), *Developing Skills to Work with Professionals: A Training Pack*, London: NCVO.

Fontana, D. (1989), *Managing Stress*, London: Routledge & Kegan Paul.

Freudenberger, H.J. and Richardson, Q. (1980), *Burnout: The High Cost of Achievement*, New York: Archer Press.

Froggatt, H. and Stamp, P. (1991), *Managing Pressure at Work*, London: BBC Books.

Hanson, P. (1990), *The Joy of Stress*, London: Pan Books.

Hartley, M. (1995), *The Good Stress Guide*, London: Sheldon Press.

Lakein, A. (1984), *How to Control your Time and your Life*, Aldershot: Gower.

Martin, M. and Smith, C. (1993), *Planning for the Future: An Introduction to Business Planning for Voluntary Organisations*, London: NCVO.

McCallum, C. (1992), *How to Raise Funds and Sponsorship*, Plymouth: How To Books Ltd.

Chapter 5: Managing volunteers as individuals

Bates, S. (1993), *Equal Opportunities in Voluntary Organisations*, London: NCVO.

Chueng-Judge, M. and Henley, A. (1994), *Equality in Action*, London: NCVO.

Hertzberg, F. (1966), *Work and the Nature of Man*, Manchester: World Publishing Co.

Knapp, M. (1990), *Time is Money: The Cost of Volunteering in Britain Today*, London: Volunteer Centre UK.

Littlewood, R. and Lipsedge, M. (1982), *Aliens and Alienists*, Harmondsworth: Penguin.

Maslow, A. (1954), *Motivation and Personality*, New York: Harper & Row.

McGregor, D. (1960), *The Human Side of Enterprise*, New York: McGraw-Hill.

Working with Refugees and Asylum Seekers (1991), League of Red Cross and Red Crescent Societies, Geneva.

Chapter 6: Volunteers in teams

Belbin, R.M. (1981), *Management Teams: Why They Succeed or Fail*, London: Heinemann.

Broome, A. (1990), *Managing Change*, London: Macmillan.

Kanter, R. Moss (1985), *The Change Masters*, New York: Allen & Unwin.

Lewin, K. (1951), *Field Theory and Social Science*, New York: Harper.

Tuckman, B.W. (1965), 'Developmental sequence in small groups', *Psychological Bulletin*, **63** (6).

Chapter 7: Attracting and keeping volunteers

Fletcher, J. (1995), *Conducting Effective Interviews*, London: Kogan Page.

Chapter 8:   Delighting the customer

Citizen Advocacy with Older People: A Code of Good Practice (1995), London: Centre for Policy on Ageing.

Crosby, P. (1979), *Quality is Free*, New York: McGraw-Hill.

Deming, W.E. (1986), *Out of the Crisis*, Boston: Massachusetts Institute of Technology.

Effective Complaints Systems (1994), The Citizen's Charter Complaints Task Force.

Lawrie, A. (1992), *Quality of Service: Measuring Performance for Voluntary Organisations*, London: NCVO.

Milne, D. and Gibbon, L. (1994), 'Quality assurance in the voluntary sector', *International Journal of Health Care and Quality Assurance*, 7 (6), pp. 16–19.

Mortiboys, R. and Oakland, J. (1991), *Total Quality Management and Effective Leadership*, London: Department of Trade and Industry.

Oakland, J. (1989), *Total Quality Management*, London: Heinemann.

Wertheimer, A. (1993), *Speaking Out: Citizen Advocacy and Older People*, London: Centre for Policy on Ageing.

Chapter 9:   Putting it all together

Senge, P. (1990), *The Fifth Discipline*, London: Century.

For useful regular reading on contemporary volunteer policy and analysis, news, jobs and courses try:

'Society Guardian', published in *The Guardian* newspaper every Wednesday.

Community Care magazine weekly by subscription
Subscription Manager
Oakfield House
Perrymount Road
Haywards Heath
West Sussex, RH16 3DH
Subscription cost: £44 per annum

A useful range of publications is also available from:

National Council for Voluntary Organisations
Regent's Wharf
8 All Saints Street
London N1 9RL
0171 713 6161

The Volunteer Centre UK
Carriage Row
183 Eversholt Street
London NW1 1BU
0171 388 9888

Index

155

Advocacy

Skills

A HANDBOOK FOR
HUMAN SERVICE PROFESSIONALS

Neil Bateman

Advocacy is a skill used by many people in human service organisations. Social workers, community medical staff and advice workers are a few who will use such skills. Advocacy is used to overcome obstacles and to secure tangible results for customers – extra money, better services and housing. Neil Bateman's book sets out a model for effective professional practice, and outlines a number of approaches to advocacy.

This is a seminal work; no other book has been published in the UK which explains how advocacy skills can be used and developed. Advocacy is becoming part of the everyday work of many people. Advocacy Skills will be a valuable handbook for anyone concerned with the rights of others.

Neil Bateman is currently a Principal Officer with Suffolk County Council, an adviser to the Association of County Councils and a visiting lecturer at the University of East Anglia.

1995   **176 pages**   **1 85742 200 7**   **£14.95**

Price subject to change without notification

arena

How to
work with
self help
groups
Guidelines for professionals

JUDY WILSON

Coping with loss, ill health and change are part of everyday life. The best support and information often comes from those who have already gone through a similar experience. Professional care is much appreciated but is only part of the help needed – self help groups are another way of getting and giving help. They provide a different form of support when help from family, friends and professionals is not enough – or not available. There are now many thousands of groups in Britain, based on many different needs.

Most professionals value self help groups, appreciating their special type of support and information. They want to work with them and are prepared to learn the best ways to do so. This book aims to help individual professionals working in health and social services to assess, extend or change how they work with self help groups on a day-to-day basis. It is a handbook, not a textbook, providing guidelines and checklists and illustrated with quotes from both professionals and members of groups.

1996   176 pages   Hbk   1 85742 289 9   £32.50
Pbk   1 85742 288 0   £14.95

Price subject to change without notification

arena